ADVANCE PRAISE

"As a former police captain involved with public safety for over forty years, I found A.W.A.R.E. to be an invaluable, potentially lifesaving guidebook to manage safety risks, prevent victimization, and protect personal safety. S. Gale Bleth professionally managed to condense twenty-five years of teaching personal safety and self-defense into this exceptional resource, with true life stories and effective, practical strategies to keep oneself safe."

—CAPTAIN DAN WILLIS (RET.), AUTHOR OF BULLETPROOF SPIRIT

"Insightful, practical, and grounded in real-world experience, A.W.A.R.E. gives first-time college students, their families, and others the tools they need to navigate campus life safely and confidently—without sacrificing independence or peace of mind. S. Gale Bleth's playbook is a smart, accessible roadmap for staying safe in all situations."

—PHIL RIBERA (RET.), POLICE CAPTAIN, MEMOIRIST, AND AUTHOR OF THE DANNY MCKENNA DETECTIVE SERIES

"Honest, eye-opening, and written for teens standing on the edge of independence, this book doesn't preach or scare—it prepares. It exposes the risks people don't talk about, the instincts you need to trust, and the awareness that can make the difference between thriving and just surviving...

"This book is an easy read with insights from someone who has real-life experience working with young adults who fell victim due to being naive to the dangers that can exist. This book is not meant to incite fear in the reader. On the contrary, it exposes them to things to consider and stories from others that are eye-opening to better prepare someone who is lacking in life experience to make good decisions... This book also gives adults a roadmap to how to make good decisions without that inner struggle that comes with making tough decisions..."

—DETECTIVE JASON WHITE, HOMICIDE DETECTIVE
WITH THE TULSA POLICE DEPARTMENT, FEATURED
IN A&E'S THE FIRST 48 SERIES

"With more than forty years as a practicing safety expert, I highly recommend Gale's book. Awareness is the number one factor in personal safety, and this book delivers."

—STUART HASKIN, AUTHOR OF GET SAFE WITH
STUART HASKIN AND FOUNDER OF GET SAFE

A.W.A.R.E.

A.W.A.R.E.

ALERT   WATCH   ASSESS   RESPOND   ESCAPE

A PERSONAL SAFETY PLAYBOOK FOR LEAVING THE NEST

S. GALE BLETH

The material in this book is intended for education. No expressed or implied guarantee of the effects of the use of the recommendations can be given nor liability taken. The author and publisher are not responsible for any injury, loss, or harm that may result from applying the ideas in this book. Use your judgment, follow the law, and seek help from qualified professionals or emergency services when needed. If you practice A.W.A.R.E. (remain Alert, Watch your surroundings, Assess situations, Respond appropriately, and Escape when necessary), you will likely reduce your risk of victimization. It's always up to you to take as many precautions as reasonably necessary to stay safe.

A.W.A.R.E.

A Personal Safety Playbook for Leaving the Nest

FIRST EDITION

ISBN   978-1-5445-5130-2   *Hardcover*
        978-1-5445-5129-6   *Paperback*
        978-1-5445-5131-9   *Ebook*
        978-1-5445-5128-9   *Audiobook*

This book is dedicated to all the young people leaving the nest.

Stay A.W.A.R.E., and stay safe.

CONTENTS

INTRODUCTION 11

1. 90 PERCENT OF YOUR SAFETY 23

2. STAY IN YOUR YELLOW 39

3. THE A.W.A.R.E. FORMULA 55

4. THE VICTIM PYRAMID 69

5. THE OTHER 10 PERCENT 85

6. FEAR IS YOUR FRIEND 103

7. BE A GOOD WITNESS 115

8. THINK LIKE A LEO 129

9. MORE LEAVING THE NEST PLAYBOOK IDEAS 143

10. NO MEANS NO 157

CONCLUSION 169

ACKNOWLEDGMENTS 173

ABOUT THE AUTHOR 175

INTRODUCTION

If you're reading this book, you may be a senior in high school, or maybe you're already a first- or second-year student in college. You may even be the parent of a high school student entering college. Wherever you are and whatever stage in life, young adulthood, you've realized it's time to become more A.W.A.R.E. about your personal safety.

I believe that people of all stages in life will benefit from becoming more A.W.A.R.E. While I will mainly focus on young adults who are leaving the nest and heading into the wild, this book is for all people.

If you are heading off for college or moving out of your family home to enter the workforce, these are big changes. When you're in high school, it's easy to be a big fish in a small pond. There are hundreds of kids on your campus, or maybe a few thousand. You probably know almost everyone in your grade; you probably grew up with many of them, and you know some of them quite well. There are groups, and you know who is in what group and why. If you're a senior, you're a big shot; you're cool.

As you near the end of your senior year of high school, you have a big change coming up. You're probably going to leave home, if not right away, then sometime soon. You might be staying close to home or going all the way across the country. You might be leaving to attend a small school or going to a larger one. Maybe you're going to a trade school or into the military. Whatever it is, you are moving on to the "real" world.

No longer can you be a big fish in the small pond of high school. No one is going to know who you are. It will be the opposite, in fact. There will be twelve thousand, twenty thousand, maybe thirty-five thousand students on your campus. You're going to be a very small fish in a very large pond. You're going to be a tiny, little guppy in the ocean.

It's time to prepare for the unknown. You're transitioning, or if you've already arrived, you have already transitioned, but you're in the midst of some very big challenges.

This is both good news and bad news. You're free from the constraints of your childhood home and family environment. You can do what you want, when you want, for the most part. You're in a whole new place, with all new people and new experiences. You get to join things and get into activities. You can eat what you want and sleep when you want. Sounds amazing, right? It will be.

However, hang on a minute before you run out the door to college (or, if you're already there, before you head out on a Friday night). Let's talk about staying safe. You're aware you'll need to use your head to get good grades and pass your classes, but are you aware that you'll also need to use your head to avoid becoming a victim of a crime?

As freeing as it might be to start fresh in a new place, don't forget that Mom and Dad are not going to be around to help you, feed you, or save you from the dangers that exist out in the larger world.

Don't forget about peer pressure. If you were a big fish in a small pond, peer pressure may have been a thing, but once you get to college, because you are no longer that big fish, the peer pressure is going to increase. In college, you have to try harder to be accepted because nobody knows you yet. The point is that you can't allow yourself to be negatively influenced by others in ways that could put you in danger. You have to be careful and make sound choices. You have to stay focused and aware of the risks involved in whatever you want to do.

What kind of risks, you may ask? For one thing, many people get their drinks spiked at college parties and college-town bars. So if you go to a party or a bar, make sure you cover your drink. Also, if you use a rideshare app to get somewhere, try and go with a friend or friends, and if you can't and have to go alone, it's best to take a screenshot of your driver and share your location with a friend along with the screenshot. You should always try to go places with other people, no matter what your mode of transportation is. There is power in numbers.

On campus, make sure your laptop or cell phone doesn't get stolen. Keep your valuables locked away and well hidden wherever they are. Unfortunately, you can't even trust your roommates, much less their friends, so don't leave valuables lying around. I worked with campus security at a university for sixteen years, and I saw many students who didn't trust their roommates. As a result, they carried their valuables around in their backpacks everywhere they went.

Do I sound a little intense? If you'd been working in campus safety, personal safety, and self-defense for twenty-five years, like I have, you'd be intense about it too. Unfortunately, I have seen a lot of crime on and around campuses. In my experience, many young people aren't being intense enough about the subject of their personal safety once they leave the nest.

I am not trying to make you paranoid. I don't want you to feel like you should just stay in your room for four years. I want you to have a great time, explore, and have adventures.

However, I want you to be aware that risky situations could present themselves. The chances are slim, but they could happen, and you need to be prepared.

You're still young, and you probably just moved out of your parents' house, or you are about to. You might be feeling some anxiety about all this. It can feel overwhelming. Compared to high school, this is going to be pretty intimidating. Again, people won't know who you are. If you're living in a dorm, you will be surrounded by a large group of new people from diverse backgrounds. So much of that is unknown, and it can be frightening.

You might be thinking, *I've never done this before. I've never been on my own like this. It'll be months before I see my parents again. How is everyone else feeling? Am I the only one freaking out?*

Probably not. It's very common for graduating high school seniors and incoming college freshmen to feel overwhelmed and anxious. Rest assured, you are not alone. That is why colleges and universities hold orientations either in person or online; these events help you learn about and adjust to your new world, making it less daunting when you show up for move-in.

It helps to get involved and join activities. It helps to create a social life with new friends. But the bottom line is that it is all going to be brand new. You will have to navigate a whole new highway.

The first time I started teaching personal safety on campus, my audience was a group of high school seniors who were incoming college freshmen. On the first day of my course, these kids were restless and out of control. I had a hard time getting their attention, but I managed to get through it. The next day, I had another group of kids and wondered how I was going to get their attention. So I got there early and sat in the back of the room. I tried to dress and act as if I were a student. I just sat there, writing in my notebook, as all the kids came in for the class. They were all broken out into different cliques, and they were all wrapped up in their own conversations. After a few minutes had passed, they started asking each other, "Hey, where's our instructor?"

I even asked them, "Does anybody know who our instructor is?"

Nobody knew. Nobody cared. They mostly just mumbled, "Whatever."

I stood up and said, "I guess I'll just teach."

I got up in front of the class and started pointing at various members of the audience. I said, "Do me a favor. You two stay there, and you go over there and sit, and then that group of four, one of you needs to go sit in each corner. Please go now."

They responded with amusement and disbelief. "You're not our instructor!" one of them said.

I said, "Yes, I am. That's why I sat in the back of the room watching you all walk in, acting like you owned the place. I need you guys to listen. This is important stuff. This is your personal safety at risk."

After that, they listened. And guess what I told them? I said, "You're about to leave high school. You're this big, cool senior; you're the 'big fish' on campus. And right now you get to pick on all the little fish, but once you're here in college, you won't be that 'big fish' anymore. You'll be tiny, little guppies in an ocean. And it's not just here in your college life but also when you are out in the real world, working in the first real job of your career."

Do I have your attention now? Good.

You're probably already aware that you're going to have to use your brain to succeed in college. Your academic life will be challenging. Whether you're going to college or into the workforce, or the military, whatever it is, you're now a young adult. You're going to have to be sharp. But what I want you to realize is that you also have to be sharp in the arena of personal safety. You have to wise up and keep your head on straight when it comes to not being a victim of a crime.

You may already have fears about leaving home and having to integrate and deal with all those new people. Even if you can't wait to leave, the fear of the unknown is a common theme for everyone.

Depending on how much responsibility and independence your parents gave you when you were growing up, you may have very little experience problem-solving out in the real world. Also, depending on how strict they were, you may be filled with anticipation and excited to take advantage of all that newfound freedom. Many kids are eager to leave, but just as many are not. You may be nervous about having to handle everything on your own. Even if you have a dorm and a food hall, there is still a lot you'll be responsible for that you probably have never had to think about before: dealing with your roommate, navigating the campus, and studying at a higher level of education, for example.

Even if you've been going to parties in high school, the college party scene will take your social life to a whole new level. You'll be introduced to many cultural differences and diversity, as well as more alcohol and drugs. You'll need to heighten your cultural sensitivity to get along with others from all over the country and world.

There's nothing wrong with leaving home—it's an important step you're taking toward maturity. The only problem is that there will be much less infrastructure for your personal safety. You won't have the comforts of home or the same level of shelter from threats. The challenges are the lack of familiarity and the lack of awareness about your surroundings on a moment-to-moment basis. This often leads to problems for first-year college students. With all of that freedom, you will be tempted to take advantage of it in ways that might be dangerous.

Since you're in a completely new environment, possibly at a very large school far away from the home you grew up in, the challenge is really to wake up. Look around and think about it. Realize that it can be wild and crazy out there. Most people are good and kind and not a threat. But there are bad apples—that's just the reality. You're on your own to start making wise choices. It is up to you and you only.

If you haven't gotten to college yet, and even if you have, this book will help you be more prepared if you find yourself in a dangerous situation. After reading this book, you'll know how to prevent yourself from becoming a victim of a crime. You'll understand the value of removing the opportunity for a crime to occur. And you'll learn how not to be vulnerable to bad things happening.

This book is here to provide you with a mindset shift: you will go from being unaware and unprepared to being A.W.A.R.E. In this book, *A.W.A.R.E.* is not just a word; it's also an acronym for a personal safety mindset:

1. Alert—Stay mentally aware of your surroundings and avoid risky situations.
2. Watch—Be on the lookout for any suspicious activity.
3. Assess—Identify the threat and take action if necessary.
4. Respond—Respond to the threat assessment; decide whether to stay or go.
5. Escape—Identify an exit route if danger arises and find safety.

It's important to stay mentally present when you are out and about. Avoid distractions like looking at your phone, especially if you're walking alone. Make wise choices about where you go, who you go with, and how you get there (we will talk more about this later in the book).

Trust your instincts! If you feel like something isn't right, move away, yell if necessary, or call authorities for help.

If you do witness a crime, report it right away. Be proactive without putting yourself in danger if you recognize suspicious activities or unsafe situations.

Empower yourself by learning self-defense techniques like the ones in this book, and get educated about all the aspects of personal safety. Get smart about it!

The goal of this book is to change your mindset about being in the world so that you can proactively avoid any risky situations. While I will share a few tactical self-defense strategies, the goal of this book is for you to never be in a position to have to use them.

It's time to wake up; it's a different world out there. In Chapter 1, I'll introduce you to a typical student named Lili. Lili is a fictional character and a composite of many high school and college-aged students I've encountered. Lili's story and the stories of others around her can help you identify the realities of jumping "out of the nest and into the wild" of college life. Hopefully, her stories will help you gain insight into how you can avoid becoming a victim of a crime.

Lili is from a midsize suburban town and grew up in a sheltered environment where crime was low and everyone knew and trusted each other. When she arrives at college, as you'll see, she is clueless about how to keep herself from becoming a victim.

You'll also meet Bri, Lili's roommate. Bri is from the big city and is street smart. She's been around the block, has seen most everything, and takes a much bolder, sometimes reckless approach to college. Although Bri understands the risks more than Lili does, she doesn't always take the steps to avoid them, and she, too, needs to get smarter about her own personal safety.

The book you're holding in your hands is here to show you how to stay safe and prevent yourself from becoming a victim. I want to help you succeed at this more than anything else. If you take anything away from this book after reading it, I hope it will be how to succeed in college (and if not in college, then in life) *and* stay safe while living on your own for the first time. The tools, tips, and reminders in this book are all designed to enlighten and empower you so that you can rock college instead of getting knocked down by it.

The solution is to open your eyes and become more aware and knowledgeable. Learn how to use only your own body as a personal weapon if necessary. Learn all of these strategies; this education will support you not just through college but also through life.

My own college years were spent at California State University, East Bay (formerly Hayward), where I received a degree in speech communication. The university did not have a large university police force, so they sent me away to a COPPS (community-oriented policing and problem-solving) training course so that I could teach the COPPS concepts in their criminal justice classes. The university police also offered a safety class for women called R.A.D.—Rape Aggression Defense—Systems.

It's a nationally known training course that is offered on many campuses in all fifty states and several countries. Before I became an instructor, I kept saying I would sign up for the class because it was important to learn self-defense, but I never could find the time as it was a twelve-hour course stretched out to four nights at three hours each. Since the R.A.D. class was offered twice a year, in the fall and spring quarters, I kept putting it off, telling myself I would sign up for the next one, until two rapes occurred on campus a few months apart. After that, I immediately signed up to take the course.

However, fate had a little surprise in store for me because instead of being enrolled in the course as a student, I was sent to San Diego for the R.A.D. Systems instructor program so that I could become an instructor. Since that time, I've been an instructor for R.A.D. Systems at universities, community colleges, private sector businesses, church groups, and private groups out in the community, and I am a huge proponent of the program.

Teaching personal safety was my passion, and it became my mission to make a difference in people's lives by changing their mindset around it. Because of this, in 2006, the Hayward Police Department hired me to work in the community policing unit for them, and I became their crime prevention specialist.

That was the beginning of a sixteen-year career in crime

prevention, which included presenting on personal safety for the Hayward community.

When I first started as a R.A.D. instructor, many of the people who I knew could benefit from it didn't have the time for the twelve-hour course, which includes physical instruction on self-defense tactics to use in case of an assault that you cannot escape from. To help those who were short on time, I created a version of the R.A.D. course that has a very limited focus on the physical motions and is instead a broader informational resource, which I called a personal safety class. From this personal safety course I developed the A.W.A.R.E. strategies that I will teach you in this book.

There are no guarantees in life and no guarantees in this book either, but what I can offer you is a very large toolbox for your personal safety at school and beyond. This isn't a training manual, although we do offer some key self-defense moves in case you find yourself unable to avoid a physical confrontation. While I draw heavily on the methods and philosophies of Rape Aggression Defense (R.A.D.) Systems, this is not a sales pitch for R.A.D. Systems or for my shortened version of it either. This book is more of a playbook to guide you and teach you viable methods to avoid being a victim of a crime.

By reading this book, you will gain tools that you can carry with you 24/7. You'll fill your toolbox with knowledge and information on topics such as avoiding risky situations (without staying in your room for four years). Once you learn and adopt these tools into your life, you'll know that you can avoid a lot of risky situations through preparation, planning, and being proactive. You'll also understand that you have options if you do end up in a risky situation and can't escape. You don't have to be a victim. You always have options; you just need to know what they are.

Personal safety training is mental. You don't necessarily need to learn jujitsu or be an MMA fighter, although those are both wonderful skills to have. But most of the work in protecting yourself from becoming a victim is not physical. In fact, as we will explore in depth throughout this book, 90 percent of your personal safety is simply about staying Alert, Watching what is happening around you, Assessing situations, Responding appropriately, and Escaping if necessary.

For decades, I've worked passionately to educate young people, especially young women, about their personal safety. I am sharing this vital information with you in this book to teach as many young people as I can how to avoid becoming a victim. That is the whole purpose of this book. The first step toward educating you is helping you to learn more about what is entailed in 90 percent of your safety, and this is what we will examine in Chapter 1: "90 Percent of Your Safety."

90 PERCENT OF YOUR SAFETY

Eighteen-year-old Lili grew up in a small suburban city east of San Francisco. She was an intelligent, ambitious student but raised in a very sheltered environment and not at all savvy about social situations. Her family was devoutly Catholic and had strict rules about what Lili could and couldn't do, so while she had friends at school and everyone liked her, she never went to parties or socialized much with other kids. Her parents couldn't afford to send her to college, so Lili studied hard to get a full-ride scholarship to an Ivy League school, where she could pursue her prelaw undergraduate degree and one day become a partner for a prestigious law firm.

Lili fulfilled her dream and was accepted at an East Coast Ivy League school. All she could think about was how awesome it would be to become a well-known, successful attorney. She was ecstatic. However, because she hadn't used the university's housing portal or a roommate finder like RoomSync or Roomsurf to match up with a roommate who was similar to her, Lili ended up sharing a dorm room with Bri, whose personality was the complete opposite of Lili's. Bri was outgoing, sociable, and a party animal from Boston. Bri was also smart, but unlike Lili, she came from a wealthy yet broken family, and she'd lived a wild life before graduating high school. Lili, on the other hand, came from a stable home with two healthy, happy, caring parents and was quite naive about the real world.

A few weeks into the first semester, Lili was challenged by her roomie, Bri, because all she wanted to do was stay out late and go to campus parties, so Lili decided it was best to avoid Bri as much as possible. Lili kept to herself and focused solely on her academics. Lili managed to get through the first semester with all A's. When the spring semester started, the Northeast region was experiencing a major snowstorm, dropping temperatures below zero degrees. Lili and Bri and the rest of the students on campus had to stay indoors for everyone's safety. By the time the sun peeked through the clouds, everyone had cabin fever, even Lili, and especially Bri.

Bri immediately started making plans to go to a party that night and asked Lili to go with her. Lili had never been to a college party and had no idea what to expect, so she hesitated, but Bri urged her to just come for a little while. Lili was tired of being cooped up during the snowstorm, and even though she knew she wouldn't really fit in with the crowd, it would be nice to meet new people, so she put on her favorite jeans and a sweater and decided to brave it.

The party was within walking distance of their dorm room at a fraternity house. When they got to the party, Bri immediately ran off to hang out with some friends and left Lili standing there by herself. Pretty soon, a guy approached her and handed her a red Solo cup with beer from the keg and asked if she wanted a drink. She stated that she didn't like beer, so he walked her over to the kitchen counter, which had been made into an improvised cocktail station. Then he turned his back to her and picked up a glass from the bar. When he turned back around, he had a cocktail in his hand and held it out to her with a smile. She sniffed it and tried not to wince—she wasn't used to the smell of alcohol. She took a sip, and she and the boy started talking. A few minutes into their conversation, Lili didn't feel right. She wasn't quite sure what was happening, and by the time the boy led her upstairs to a bedroom, she was feeling the effects of the Rohypnol he had put in her drink. She had been "roofied" and blacked out.

Lili woke up in her dorm room the next morning with no memory of how she'd gotten home or what had happened at the party. Bri told her that she'd brought her home after finding her asleep upstairs in one of the bedrooms. Lili was mortified and wondered what had happened. She felt sore with heavy cramping and was bleeding, and she wondered why, since her period wasn't coming for a few weeks. She felt sick from the alcohol, and her memory was foggy. She just figured she had no memory of what happened because she'd had too much to drink.

Lili put that evening out of her mind and tried to forget what had happened. She wanted to crawl under a rock and hide until she felt better and then never go to a party again. After a few days, Lili went back to focusing on her classes until, one day, she realized that she was several weeks late for her period. Soon, a pregnancy test confirmed that she was pregnant. Lili was overwhelmed with shock and extremely embarrassed. She told no one. But since she came from a strict Catholic family, she would eventually take a leave of absence from school to carry the baby to term and then put it up for adoption before resuming her studies at a different university.

Lili left the comfort and safety of her parents' nest and went into an environment that was unknown to her. She was naive and unaware of other dangers she would encounter in the world of a university campus, which led her to drink a cocktail that was laced with Rohypnol and become pregnant. Her dreams of being a successful attorney were derailed, at least for the next nine months of her young life. Her unfortunate story is a scary but true example of why 90 percent of your personal safety is in your head, and by this, I mean the more information, knowledge, and awareness you have, the less likely you are to become a victim of a crime.

If Lili could take that night back, what would she do differently? Well, if she had read this book, she would know how to handle herself at a party, especially a college party with a lot of alcohol and drugs. She would understand how to deal with being around people she doesn't know or trust. Lili would not have accepted a drink from someone if she did not directly watch them make it. She would have known that once she had her drink, she should protect it at all times. But there are other mistakes she made that she can't take back. And they all amount to not using her head due to lack of being A.W.A.R.E.

THE A.W.A.R.E. FORMULA

Ninety percent of your safety lies in these five things: Alert, Watch, Assess, Respond, and Escape. If you're in your late teens or early twenties, or any age, you know that when you go to a party, there will be alcohol and probably drugs, and you should expect that there will be some level of risk. Because you know this, you should always be on alert. You watch for anything that looks suspicious, assess any situation if something doesn't look or feel right, formulate your response if you're going to stay, or plan an escape if that's the best option.

Get all the information without sounding paranoid: You can say, "A party? That sounds like fun! Where is it? What's the vibe going to be like?" Whatever the response is, in the back of your mind, what you are really gathering is information that will keep you alert about the risks involved. You're really asking questions like "Where is it? Who is the host? What kind of kids are they? How many people are supposed to be there? What kind of alcohol or drugs might be at the party? How will we get there, and more importantly, how will we get home?"

You have already committed to attending. You'll hear me say this numerous times in this book: when you leave the nest, you must stay alert at all times. Only you can keep yourself safe. The world is full of great and beautiful things, but it is also full of dangerous situations. You need to watch out. Watching is simply observing and noticing everything in your surroundings. Right now, you are reading this book or listening to it. Look around you. Take it all in. What do you see? What details can you absorb? Are there any potential dangers in your environment? If not, then great, you can relax.

You need to be armed with not just information but also the experience and common-sense knowledge to know what to do with that information. If you know that parties held by a certain group of people are usually full of drunk and high people who are likely to make bad decisions, be very careful when going to them, keep them to a minimum, or stay away from them entirely. I will discuss what Lili could have done below.

Unfortunately, Lili did not know any of this before she went to the party. If she'd read this book, she could say to herself, *Wait, I'm going to a house party with college kids, and they'll all be like Bri*. Lili could have used A.W.A.R.E. to keep herself safe.

She would be *alerted* that she was going to a place where she'd never been in her life. She was going to attend a party with people she'd been avoiding since she arrived. They would be indulging in things she didn't do, like alcohol and drugs. It would be loud, a bit crazy, and outside of her comfort zone.

Once there, she could *watch* for any dangerous situations that could potentially harm her. She would have looked into the dangers of college parties and known about the chances of getting her drink spiked. She would have ensured that she watched over her beverage at all times.

As she was enjoying the party, she would also scan the room to make her own *assessment* of the people there and their actions.

If the party was full of wall-to-wall kids with extremely loud music, and a joint or a bong was being passed around, not to mention if there was a beer pong game in the living room, then Lili would have *responded* with a decision of whether she wanted to stay or go back to the dorm.

If she wanted to stay and brave it out, then she would be watchful of what she drank. If she didn't want to stay, she would leave the party and quietly make her *escape*.

At all times, she would be thinking these things through, recognizing and preparing for anything that might potentially happen to her.

This is risk recognition, and it leads to risk reduction. When you're practicing risk reduction, you're aware of the risks and you reduce them as much as possible. You arrive at a party, and when someone introduces himself to you and offers to get you a drink, you insist on going with him to the keg. Maybe you tell him sorry, you don't drink beer, so he offers to go make you a cocktail. He tells you he'll make you a concoction you'll love, something sweet.

He starts to turn at an angle so you can't really see what he's doing, and you realize he might put something in your drink, so you say, "Wait. No, let me see what you're doing." If you didn't see your drink being made, just walk outside and pretend to accidently spill it, and just say that you will help yourself to a bottled water. This kind of active, preventive behavior doesn't simply allow risky things to happen to you. You are in charge of your personal safety; you make smart decisions and act wisely.

AVOIDING THEFT ON CAMPUS

Of course, you need to be careful in many other places besides parties. When you leave the nest, most often you'll end up having roommates, and this means you'll be living with strangers, at least until you get to know them. Most students have never lived with any other kids besides their siblings. Especially if you're an only child, like Lili was, you might be intimidated by the idea of meeting new people or worried about whether they are trustworthy or not. After working at a university for sixteen years, I've seen enough incidents to know that you can't always trust your roommates or dormmates. Take time to get to know people before you trust them. Again, you don't have to be paranoid, just A.W.A.R.E.

This book isn't about trust, but it is about protecting yourself by using A.W.A.R.E. In the case of judging whether you can trust your roommates, start gathering information as soon as you meet them. Get to know them and stay alert by using your knowledge and experience to get a sense of their character and trustworthiness. Process that information and decide how you feel about someone and what your thoughts are about them, based on what you know. Some of this can come from questions you ask, and some of it might be a matter of just observing the other person and getting a sense of their background and values.

You also need to continually watch who is around you and what is happening around you. Try not to get so distracted by everything new and exciting and fun the school has to offer that you fall out of a state of relaxed alertness.

Many people head off for college with no clue about how rampant theft is on most campuses. For instance, university libraries have a high degree of theft. If you're in the library studying and you have to go to the bathroom, don't just walk away from your laptop. Assess your situation. You don't have to pack up all your stuff and risk losing your spot at a table, but you can ask someone nearby if they can keep an eye on your valuables, saying something like "Do you mind watching my stuff? I need to use the restroom." Libraries have tons of expensive electronics lying around out in the open, and thieves know this. Many libraries have cameras now to prevent crime, but just because there's a camera, there's still no guarantee your stuff won't get stolen. You don't want to take that chance, right? Even if they do have cameras, do you want the stress and headache of dealing with reporting the crime and trying to recover your laptop? Whether you're in the library, the dorm, the food court, or virtually anywhere on campus, after you assess your surroundings, respond to any risk by either finding someone to watch your valuables or taking all your belongings with you.

TWO SIDES OF AWARENESS

There are two kinds of awareness you need to have: external awareness and internal awareness. External awareness is just what it sounds like: staying aware of your surroundings. Who is around you? What is happening? What do you see, hear, or smell? Internal awareness is how you feel inside about something. Do you have a gut feeling that someone is not trustworthy or that a situation you're about to get yourself into might be dangerous?

Being aware externally is something you can learn. It involves actions such as not leaving your purse in your car, sitting out for all to see. It means not getting too close to someone who is clearly drunk or angry. It's about learning to keep your eyes open and think about what you see and what others can see as well. If you see that the person walking toward you looks suspicious or just doesn't look right, or you hear people yelling and screaming at each other, leave the area. These are clear signs you should put some distance between yourself and what could be a potentially dangerous situation.

These two kinds of awareness, internal and external, are interdependent. External awareness often leads to internal awareness and vice versa. You see something or hear something, and your gut starts to feel strange about it. You might wonder what is going on. Sometimes, however, things can appear harmless on the outside but are actually dangerous on the inside. Your gut can help you in those times as well.

In the book *The Gift of Fear*, by Gavin de Becker, the author tells a story of a woman who encountered a nice-looking man outside her apartment building. He offered to help her carry her groceries up to her apartment. He seemed like a friendly, helpful passerby, and her groceries were heavy, so after a bit of hesitation, she agreed to let him help her upstairs. The minute they got to her door and she opened it, he forced his way in. Once inside, he raped her. Afterward, he got up to shut the window before he stepped out. He said he was just going to the kitchen for a glass of water, but something told her that if she didn't leave right that second, she would die, and so she took the opportunity to escape. She could barely move, but she got out the door and slipped into a neighbor's apartment.

Before she let him come upstairs, she had a gut feeling that something wasn't right and considered saying no, but she ignored her intuition. The second time, she listened when "something told her" to act.

Sometimes your gut tells you that something isn't quite right, but your mind tries to convince you that it is. You talk yourself out of it, which is what this woman did at first. This is a common behavior, and many aren't even in touch with their intuition enough to recognize when something seems wrong.

In my experience, in Hayward, sometimes people will be lying on the ground next to their bicycle on the street or in a parking lot, and it will appear that they have fallen off their bike. A few times, they have done this just to lure someone out of their vehicle so they can rob them. People driving by will stop, thinking someone's hurt and they need to get out and help them, and the next thing they know, they're being robbed or carjacked. A similar thing often happens in gas stations. Someone is getting gas, and someone comes up and talks to them while they're pumping gas. Meanwhile, their accomplice sneaks over to the driver's side of the car and steals their purse or wallet. I have seen a lot of cases of this, so I personally lock up my car and keep my keys with me when I'm filling up at the gas station. If someone wants to come talk to me, they can talk to me. But they're not getting in my car.

GO WITH YOUR GUT, NO MATTER WHAT

I always tell people to go with their gut, no matter what. And what our mothers always told us is really true: never trust a stranger. No matter how bright and cheery things may seem, if something occurs to you "in the back of your mind," listen to it. Even if you're thinking, *I know I shouldn't be doing this, but I'm sure it'll be okay*, you shouldn't be doing it. We will explore much more about the ways fear can be our greatest teacher in Chapter 6, but for now, understand the importance of staying aware of both what's outside of you and what's going on inside of you.

Awareness can also lead to knowledge and information. Because I just gave you this information about the bicycle trick, now you can use your knowledge if you become aware of a guy on the ground with his bike, looking like he just fell. You'll stay in your car, and you'll call 911 and say something like "There's a guy who seems to have fallen off his bike, and he looks hurt, but I don't trust the neighborhood I'm in, so please send an officer to come check on him."

Your heart may tell you to help him out, but your gut knows it could be dangerous. Up to this point, you stayed alert, watched what was happening, assessed the situation, and ultimately responded to your assessment that this guy on the ground might not be safe. Your parents may have taught you to help others, and so you want to help this person lying on the ground. He seems to be hurt. But you also have an external awareness that this may not be a safe situation, because you're in a crime-ridden neighborhood. He could be trying to trick you. You don't need to just leave him there; you can call for help. We will keep coming back to this idea that helping a stranger may not always be a wise choice. Sometimes it can lead to you becoming a victim of theft or even assault. If someone needs help, call 911. They will route the call to the paramedics or police, depending on the situation.

KNOWLEDGE VERSUS INFORMATION

What's the difference between knowledge and information? Knowledge comes from your personal experiences, whereas information comes from what you've heard or read or seen happening to others. Let's say you have the information that if you leave your valuables unattended in the library, gym, or food court, there is a possibility they will be stolen.

This information can lead to the awareness that you need to keep an eye on your belongings in public places. It also means you remain aware of your surroundings and the people who are around you. When you're in that experience of successfully keeping your things safe, you gain the knowledge you need to avoid becoming a victim.

Personal safety is about making wise choices and taking precautions. In order to make those wise choices and take those precautions, you need to be informed, and sometimes the best way to get informed is the obvious way: do some research. Universities today are required to make the records of all crimes on campus and in the areas near the campus public information. You can find that information on any campus website by searching for the school's annual security report, which all accredited institutions are mandated to publish by the Jeanne Clery Campus Safety Act. The ASR will detail all incidents of reported crimes on campus for the past three years. If you're leaving home but not going to a college campus, finding an apartment and working instead, you can do the same thing. Most cities have crime reports by neighborhood, where you can find statistics on theft, assault, and other crimes.

When I started working at the Hayward Police Department, I was in shock and disbelief to learn how much crime was happening in the city I lived in. I thought the university had its share of criminal activity; however, the crimes in the city were far worse: homicides, robberies, burglaries, carjacking, high speed chases that turned deadly, assault, road rage, and much more. I thought those things were just in the movies. I didn't have the information about this when I started out because I hadn't done my research.

Research the statistics on crime for the college you attend or plan to attend, and examine the places on and near campus where the most crime occurs. Ask questions like "What kinds of crimes are most common? What places would be best to avoid?"

Information is only a start. You also need to use that information properly by always staying aware of your surroundings. For example, a friend of mine was in a fraternity when he was in college. His frat house was off campus, and one night they were having a party. Some people who were locals, not students, showed up to crash the frat party. My friend heard a commotion outside and walked out to see what was going on and walked into the middle of a fight. The next thing he knew, he had been punched in the face and knocked unconscious. He had to be carried back into the house by his frat mates, who later told him what had happened. If he had raised his awareness about the scene outside the house, perhaps by looking out a window or listening from inside before he stepped outside, he could have avoided that painful punch.

Hate crimes have also become an issue on and around some colleges. Whether for religious, gender, or political reasons, campuses are known to be places where vocalizing opinions is common. Campuses are supposed to be safe places for free speech, but sometimes protests can get out of hand and become unsafe. If you see signs of any potentially violent or aggressive people who are singling out a section of the population or shouting hate messages, steer clear of the scene. Keep your distance as much as possible because there's no way to know what could happen with that level of tension. If you feel it's appropriate, call campus security or local police to inform them of what you are witnessing.

JUST LEAVE

It sounds simple, but the primary message of this book is this: if you find yourself in a risky situation, *leave*. Just leave. Take in the details and descriptions of people and vehicles as much as you safely can, in case you need to be a witness, but don't do anything that might endanger you. If something suspicious is going on, and you can feel the intensity of a crowd or an angry confrontation of some kind, don't get in the middle of it. Your goal is to escape because you never know how bad a situation might get. Get out of there, and then when you're safe, call for help.

If Lili had read this book before Bri invited her to the party, she would have been much more informed and aware, both externally, by noticing all the drunk people at the party and refusing to take a drink made by a stranger, and internally, by listening to her gut about the potential risks of drinking what the guy was offering her. She would have resisted the peer pressure and maybe chosen not to go to the party in the first place. If you find yourself in a similar situation, don't take a drink from someone unless you directly see it being prepared. You can find a sealed bottle of water or an unopened can of soda and drink that instead. Don't leave your drink sitting around where someone can put something in it, and definitely don't drink out of a punch bowl or similar trough-like container.

Ninety percent of your safety is in prevention. This means avoiding any opportunities for victimization. The best way to do this is through the A.W.A.R.E. mindset—stay Alert, Watch, Assess, Respond, and Escape. Armed with these five actions, you're likely to never get to the other 10 percent, which is when you find yourself in an altercation or being physically robbed or assaulted. At that point, the goal becomes to escape. If it's not possible, then you have to use your own personal weapons that are on your body, which I'll explain later in the book. These basic self-defense moves can help you disable the assailant enough so that you can escape.

I hope you've come to see that when you're in a state of A.W.A.R.E., you are in the optimal mindset for safety. You are calm yet alert. This relaxed but still watchful way of being is just one of five different states of awareness on the spectrum of the Color Code of Awareness. It is the safest state to be in, as you'll learn, and that is what we will explore in the next chapter, "Stay in Your Yellow."

CHAPTER 1: STAY A.W.A.R.E. TAKEAWAYS

- The goal is always to escape.
- Be informed about potential risks nearby.
- Stay aware of your surroundings and your gut feelings.

STAY IN YOUR YELLOW

What happened to Lili was extremely sad, especially since it could have been avoided. When she agreed to go to the party, she didn't bother to ask Bri for any advice or learn more about who was throwing it and what kind of kids might be there. She was ignorant about all of that, and worse, when she got to the party, she was not at all alert to the risks involved with taking a drink someone else had brought her. She did not realize that the number one rule at parties and bars is to never drink something that could be spiked with a drug of some kind. The number two rule is related—never leave your drink unattended. Always have it covered with a napkin. If you take anything from reading this book, I hope it's those two things.

If you black out, you won't be able to use any of the other information in this book. If you black out, you're literally not in control of what you're doing and will not remember anything when the drug wears off, just like Lili. And as it turned out, when she woke up in the morning, she was unwilling to consider the possibility that she had been a victim of a crime.

She was so terrified she might have been sexually assaulted that she didn't even want to think about it. Instead, she tried to put it out of her mind completely. She was so overwhelmed by fear that she went into denial.

As it turns out, black is also the last color on the Color Code of Awareness, and it represents "complete panic that renders us useless." This is the freeze response, when instead of fleeing or fighting, we are paralyzed.

To explain the Color Code of Awareness, I'll start with a story. Several years ago, I was in Monterey, California, at the Laguna Seca racetrack, watching an IndyCar event with some friends on a Sunday afternoon. The race was over, and we were driving back up to Hayward. One way out of the Laguna Seca racetrack was through a former army base called Fort Ord, which at the time had just transitioned into a new campus for Cal State University, Monterey Bay. To me, it looked strange because it was a former army base, and I was familiar with a military base, as I grew up a military brat from the time I was born until I graduated high school. So I was driving around, trying to find the on-ramp to the freeway, but while doing that, I couldn't help but notice these wooden signs on every street corner with the engravement of a specific color on all of them. I found myself driving around some of the streets, and still the same color was on all signs. Then I snapped out of it and realized we were lost inside the base or university.

A campus police officer saw me driving suspiciously around and around and lit me up! The officer asked us nicely, "May I ask what you're doing here?"

I told him we were lost and couldn't find our way to the freeway, so he gave us directions. One of my friends who was in the car was a campus police officer at CSU East Bay, and he happened to know this CSU Monterey Bay officer who pulled me over. So before I pulled away, I decided to ask him the burning question of what the heck all those signs were for. He explained that they were currently displaying our country's threat level. I thanked him and thought to myself, *That's a lot of signs to let the base know our country's current threat level.*

I didn't think any more about it until two days later, when the attacks of 9/11 occurred. After seeing the devastation on TV and praying for those lives lost and our country's safety, I thought of those threat-level signs. I thought to myself, *Our country's threat level has changed, and all those signs will have to change as well.* You think of the strangest things in times of crisis, and I remember thinking, *Who is going to change all of our country's threat-level signs on that base?*

Color codes are used across many organizations, and there is a universal pattern to them. The United States has five levels of color we use to designate the urgency of a threat: green, blue, yellow, orange, and red.

I have learned in my years of self-defense training that we all have an internal Color Code of Awareness. Animals as well. Our three main codes are Yellow, Orange, and Red, with Red being the highest level, leading to a flight, fight, freeze, or fawn response.

THE UNIVERSAL COLOR CODE

Many organizations use color codes to coordinate their responses to emergencies. Earthquakes, tornadoes, and hurricanes all have a color code to identify the threat level. Fire departments also have their own color codes that correspond to the danger levels during fire seasons and the amount of humidity in the air as well as wind conditions. There are broad consistencies among all of the different kinds of color codes.

Red is always the highest danger level, and yellow, green, or blue is at the bottom. Even a stoplight's colors are based on the color code of green is safe and red is not when it comes to crossing an intersection.

Every human and every animal has threat levels within. Our nervous systems instinctively know when danger is approaching and when it is safe.

In the book *Principles of Personal Defense*, the author, Jeff Cooper, presents Cooper's Color Code of Awareness, which label human beings' awareness of threat levels:

White: Unaware / unprepared / easily startled

Yellow: Relaxed / alert / cautious / this is baseline awareness

Orange: Specific threat alert / heightened awareness / change in stance and behavior

Red: Immediate danger / fight-or-flight / active self-defense

Black: Complete panic / freeze / breakdown of physical and mental performance

Cooper's book was originally written for the military, but it applies to any organization with safety concerns and all human beings. In the US government's Homeland Security Advisory System, green is for safety, blue is guarded, yellow is elevated, orange is high, and red is severe. The colors may vary slightly across different uses, but the purpose is the same.

These are all large-scale color code systems, but on a much smaller scale, we all have this system within us. Most people don't know this. You have a color code inside of you that manages your awareness of threats. Your internal color code is how you know that right now, while you're reading this book, you're in a relaxed state and you're safe. You're in your Yellow Color Code. But if you hear an explosion outside of your house, now you will go into your Orange Color Code and investigate what that loud explosion was. If you see that it was your neighbor fixing his car and the engine made a loud explosion sound, then you will return back to your color code of Yellow and return to reading this book. However, if you see that people are running away from something outside, then your color code will change to Red.

You can use the Color Code of Awareness to navigate in the wild now that you've moved out of the nest. Young adults who want to protect themselves can use the color codes to raise awareness of their surroundings and recognize the threat levels so that they can take the appropriate actions.

Unfortunately, Lili was never alert or aware enough of the danger she was in while in her Yellow Color Code. She didn't realize there could be a risk until it was too late; she was completely oblivious to the hazards of accepting that drink. The next morning, when she woke up, she was confused and overwhelmed, and she put it out of her mind. She just wanted to act as if nothing had happened and take some time to heal.

Most people don't realize that there are different levels of threat awareness inside them. The idea is to make choices as you go about your daily life that allow you to always stay calm and thoroughly aware of your situation. Your goal is to stay in your Yellow Color Code and know what to do when you feel your color code is changing. Once you identify what color you're in, you'll act appropriately, whether that means staying in your Yellow Color Code or moving into an Orange Color Code or your Red Color Code. What's important is recognizing it and acting on it.

Let's say you're walking out of a coffee shop, enjoying your iced triple-shot white mocha cappuccino in your Yellow Color Code of relaxed alertness, and outside the coffee shop you find a crowd of people all gathered on a street corner, making a lot of noise. You realize this isn't just some people watching a group performing a flash mob; it's something more serious. You're going to move into your Orange Color Code because something is going on and you don't want to walk right into it. You assess the situation and walk away to escape. Then you escape the situation, return to your Yellow Color Code, and continue to enjoy your coffee drink. Whenever you fall out of your Yellow Color Code, it's a sign you need to do something. Usually, that is to leave the area if possible.

People who are in their White Color Code are intentionally ignoring a potential danger. For example, some people don't like to get annual health exams because they don't want to know if there's anything seriously wrong with them. They don't want to hassle with making life changes to better their health when the doctor tells them to, so they wait until something drastic happens and they are in need of medical care for the rest of their life. Then they go into their Black Color Code, unable to cope with it due to their fear and overwhelm from now drastically having to change their lifestyle to stay alive.

Preparedness is the key to success. People who know that but don't want to take the action to be proactive and prepared are the ones that are in the White Color Code. They are completely unprepared to take action. They will be startled and surprised and ineffective if danger strikes. This puts them in their Black Color Code. They will panic and have a mental and physical breakdown. Being either in the White Color Code or Black Color Code will not support their personal safety.

FACING REALITY

If you've experienced an earthquake, you know how literally jolting it is and how quickly your emotional state shifts when the ground is shaking beneath you. When I was a building safety assistant at CSU East Bay, I led people in earthquake drills and preparation. The Hayward Fault was what everyone in the East Bay, where a lot of my family and friends lived, feared, as the faultline ran underneath. The fault is overdue for an earthquake. They say it will probably shift soon. Shortly after I was trained to be a building safety assistant, I wanted to make sure my family was prepared when the earthquake happened. So I gathered my family together and assigned everyone a task to help them prepare a "go bag." In case of any emergency, earthquake, or fire, if we need to evacuate, everyone will have their own backpack, which will be placed in their cars or workplace. One of my family members worked for a dental office; she was going to bring everybody toothbrushes and toothpaste for their backpacks. My brother was in charge of getting water for everyone to put in their backpacks. Everyone was given a task along these lines. Once everyone had their "go bags" filled, I talked to the family about a plan B. I mentioned that we should all have a meeting place and also have a route to drive or walk in case the overpass collapses and cars can't get through.

While going over the potential dangers: fires, looters, and loss of cell service, water, and electricity for approximately three to five days, a few of my family members grew frightened and were almost in a fetal position on the couch, unwilling to listen or participate anymore. They insisted we not talk about it; they did not want to know. One family member predicted that she wouldn't be able to sleep that night since she was so scared. Because she was frozen, overwhelmed with fear, she was in her Black Color Code. She didn't want to face it even though she knew very well that the danger was there. This meant she wasn't mentally prepared. The purpose of the family meeting wasn't to scare anyone; it was just to face the reality that an earthquake will happen whether we want it to or not. Whether we accept this reality or not, we are going to be in the thick of it at some point. Have a "go bag" and be prepared. The same is true if you live in a hurricane, tornado, or wildfire zone.

I was giving my relatives the opportunity to learn all about the strategies for safety and survival preparation. Know where your gas line is located outside, and have a wrench there so you can turn off your gas line. Keep a pair of shoes under your bed because if an earthquake happens while you are sleeping, there is going to be broken glass from the windows on the floor. Along with your shoes, you should have a pair of gloves and a flashlight as well. So before you check to see if everyone in the house is okay, put your shoes on, then your gloves, and turn on your flashlight. Otherwise, you will just be another injured person that needs saving instead of being able to help others. Everyone in your family or your household of roommates should have the same kind of box under their bed. This way, you can make sure that everyone is prepared and will stay safe.

WHEN COLOR CODES SHIFT IN AN INSTANT

I was once at a law enforcement training school, watching a video of an active shooting inside a building. The video shows a group of people in a large room with cubicles, and when the video starts, they are all in their Yellow Color Code, working away. Then, all of a sudden, something happens. They hear something like popping sounds, and the people start to become alert. They move into their Orange Color Code, and when they see people starting to run in one direction, the others see the frightened expressions on their coworkers' faces and realize there is danger in the building. They have gone from an Orange Color Code to a Red Color Code and are running in the same direction as everyone else. They reach the end of the hallway with nowhere else to go, so they lock themselves in a conference room, and the shooter is trying to get into the room. When that happens, everyone gathers together to barricade the door. They move all the tables, shelving, and chairs up against the door to keep the shooter from entering. Everyone in the room is still in their Red Color Code and exhausted by all their efforts to stay safe because now they are going to have to fight for their lives when the barricade gives way.

An interesting outcome of this exercise was that some of the people went into their Red Color Code, but others went into their Black. They didn't want to move from under their desks, but they had to, or else the shooter would kill them, and there was a way out they could take. They had to escape somehow. But some of them were so frozen, so deep in their Black Color Code, that they were afraid to move. They couldn't leave. A woman in the video had to leave another woman under her desk because she was frozen, even though the shooter was right down the hall and still far enough for them to escape. The woman realized that she, too, was going to be dead, just like her coworker, if she didn't get out, so left her coworker there and managed to escape.

I personally could evaluate their color codes just by watching these people move through the different levels. Part of that recognition comes from my years of experience, but you can recognize your color codes and other people's color codes, too, because this awareness is connected to your intuition. Your gut usually knows instinctually how bad a threat is.

An overly intense shift of your emotional state and your

mindset can make things worse. For instance, if you have to slam on your brakes to avoid hitting a child on their bike with your car, your blood pressure will rise immediately, and you might be shaken up for a bit afterward. You may not drive as skillfully as you were before you were rattled by the incident. In these cases, it's important to find a way to calm down by taking deep breaths. Try pulling over and taking a few minutes to collect yourself.

SEEING RED

On the other hand, some people who could stay in their Yellow Color Code will allow themselves to get taken over by irrational levels of panic and get into their Red Color Code. This could lead them into more trouble than if they'd just stayed in their Yellow Color Code.

My sister demonstrated this some years back. I have two older sisters, and even though I've been teaching self-defense classes for twenty-five years, neither of them has taken my class—yet. One Thanksgiving, one of my sisters and I had procrastinated shopping for our Thanksgiving gathering and decided that shopping the night before the holiday would be best, since no one would be out late. We decided to go to the grocery store at around 10:00 p.m. We went to the local Safeway, and parking was a madhouse! I can't remember if it was my brilliant idea or my sister's to think that the twenty-four-hour Safeway would be completely free of last-minute shoppers. The place was packed with last-minute shoppers—everyone in the neighborhood was there, doing the same thing we were. Surprisingly, we managed to find two shopping carts, which we needed because we were hosting twenty-five people and needed a lot of food! The store was crazy crowded, and everyone in there was grabbing yams and marshmallows and canned pumpkin like we were. We looked at each other and realized this had been a bad idea. However, we had all those people coming, expecting a feast.

We both filled our carts and got in line. Every cashier station was open, and all the lines were so long that they went down the aisles. In the evening hours, the store locks one of the entrances and there is only one entrance and exit point. At the exit area that night, there was a man standing there, extremely intoxicated or with possible mental issues. He was swearing and yelling at everyone as they entered and exited the store. He made the doorway feel uncomfortable and intimidating for people going in and out of the grocery store. His voice escalated at times, and people would just look at him. My sister was watching him like a hawk. I was aware he was there, but I was flipping through the pages of a magazine. I felt the slightest possibility that he could be dangerous, but it didn't seem likely. There were a lot of people around—how much could he do? I remained calm and in my Yellow Color Code.

My sister, on the other hand, hung on to her cart, white-knuckled, going quickly from Yellow Color Code to Orange Color Code. I continued checking out the pages of the magazine, searching for something we could make for dessert.

My sister said, urgently, "Dude, do you see that guy?" I looked over, and of course I already knew there was a crazy guy over there. I was still alert but relaxed—because he seemed harmless. He wasn't getting in anyone's face; he was just yelling idiotic things.

When we were checking out, my sister went into her Black Color Code. She didn't want to move and definitely didn't want to walk by him. She was afraid he would lunge at her. I looked around at my surroundings and said, "I think we're okay. Let's just walk by. He might yell, but I think we're okay."

I calmly told my sister that his guy was obviously harmless. In my opinion, he was not scary. He was just talking, not being physically aggressive at all. But my sister's voice was filled with fear. The man behind us in line was tall, well built, and well dressed. He and his wife both appeared to be professionals. He noticed how scared my sister was, and out of the corner of my eye, I saw him leave his wife's side and walk over to the doorway and start talking to the crazy guy. I realized he was trying to distract the guy so my sister and I could pass by without a problem. So I said to my sister, "Let's go now!" and I started to walk ahead of my sister with my cart.

My sister must not have seen the tall man who was behind us go over to talk to the guy, because she suddenly ran by me at full speed with her cart, running for her life to our car. Instead of the guy ignoring her, now he was noticing that she was afraid of him, which is exactly what he wanted people to be.

I couldn't believe what I was seeing! I was running behind her and said, "You have completely lost your goddamn mind!" As she was shoving groceries in the car, she yelled, "Let's just get the f*ck out of here!"

Because she wasn't truly aware of her surroundings, she wasn't alert, watching, assessing, or responding to any of the things that I was. She didn't realize that the man behind us was distracting the crazy guy so he wouldn't bother us. She just bolted, scared to death of a harmless mentally ill person. She was sure she was going to be attacked and killed on the night before Thanksgiving. Instead of realizing there was just a strange guy at the grocery store, she raced right by me at one hundred miles an hour. I should also note that she rarely ever runs anywhere.

If you're not aware of your surroundings or your situation, you will find yourself in this fight-or-flight situation in which you feel you just need to get out fast to survive. This is where my sister was, and it was unnecessary. I know because I was thinking clearly, and I was in my Yellow Color Code, while she was acting like a lunatic. She had gone into her Red Color Code for no reason.

Some time after this, I said to her, "You know, if you had taken my class, maybe you would have handled our shopping experience a little differently."

"No, probably not," she answered. She didn't care, and she didn't want to learn more about things like situational awareness. Unfortunately, this is the case for many people... they would rather not know. Don't let this be you. When you sense risk or danger, respond appropriately. Determine the level of threat. Maybe, at the most, I could have gone into a borderline Yellow Color Code or to the low end of the Orange Color Code. But that's as far as it should have reasonably gone.

INTUITION AND COLOR CODES

How can we tell what color code we are in? Often it's just instinctual. You'll feel a physical sensation, perhaps. Police officers often talk about the hair on the back of their neck rising when they sense something is not right. They know they have to listen to their gut.

Everyone has an internal color code, and for all of us, our intuition plays a part in our awareness and our actions. You intuitively know how to respond in any particular situation. If your intuition says, *If I don't leave right now, I may die*, then leave at all costs. If your intuition says, *That guy looks possibly dangerous; I'm going to stay clear*, then stay clear and stay alert.

Intuition has a natural connection to your internal color code. It just happens without you trying. You have gut feelings, and you can use your gut feelings to figure out what color you are in or need to be in. You can ask, *Do I feel in my gut that something really bad is about to happen? Does this call for me to go into my Orange Color Code and get away or into my Red Color Code and prepare to fight?*

Reactions to fear are physical. They can be felt in your body in this range, from a White Color Code to a Yellow Color Code to an Orange Color Code to a Red Color Code to a Black Color Code. You could be sitting at your desk and hear a loud explosion outside. Your heart rate will increase a bit. You could be walking down the street and notice that someone is following you. You will walk more quickly and look for an escape route. These reactions happen without us even having to think about them. They are intuitive and instinctual.

Intuition points the way toward action. When you experience fear, your awareness is heightened and your intuition alerts you to figure out what to do. Do you just give up and hide under a desk and get killed? Or do you do everything in your power to escape? We will discuss a lot more about intuition in a later chapter, but it's helpful to realize that intuition can play a part in staying aware of your color codes.

It's all about having situational awareness. Be aware of what color code you're in, and figure out what you need to do to get back to your Yellow Color Code.

Take the time to think about how you can avoid a risky situation. This way, you can stay in your Yellow Color Code. At any time of day, you can always stop for a minute and feel your internal color code. It's always there, and in today's world, with all of the options to stay out of trouble, it is possible to stay in your Yellow Color Code most, if not all, of the time.

AWARENESS IS INSTINCTUAL

Right now, as you're reading this, you're in your Yellow Color Code. But if you hear a car alarm go off and then hear angry shouting outside, then you might get into your Orange Color Code to stay on higher alert and make sure you're safe. But if you hear gunshots instead of shouting, then you should go into your Red Color Code. You will be in self-defense mode. You're calling 911, running away, or locking your doors and windows and hiding under the bed until it's over. You're protecting your life.

Right now, as I'm writing this, I'm in my Yellow Color Code. But if an earthquake had hit earlier, I would have been in my Orange Color Code. If the house is shaking and the ground is shaking, I'll be on high alert, looking for dangers such as things falling on top of me. There's no person here endangering me, but it's still an unsafe situation, and I'm going to stay tuned in to my color code.

Now that you know this, you can use the Color Code of Awareness to identify when you are at risk and how serious the risk is. Be vigilant. Stay aware of your surroundings and aware of what's going on inside of you in terms of any stress or anxiety level changes. What's going on with your emotional state? Is something concerning going on around you that is causing you to react?

The guidance here is simple: stay aware of what color you're in and know what to do to get back to your Yellow Color Code. To do this, make choices that allow you to always stay calm and thoroughly aware of your surroundings.

I'll never forget that day at Laguna Seca when I first saw all of those wooden threat-level signs. Of course, the horrific events of 9/11 happened two days later, which certainly made it stick in my mind. But the fact is that color codes play an important role in protection, whether it's our country or our own lives.

In the next chapter, I'll share with you another approach to your personal safety—one that breaks down the word *A.W.A.R.E.* and explores the acronym I've been introducing here that can help you stay Alert, Watch, Assess the situation, Respond to a threat, and Escape if necessary. The combination of these five plans of action will help you stay in your Yellow Color Code at least 90 percent of the time.

CHAPTER 2: STAY A.W.A.R.E. TAKEAWAYS

- Color codes are used by many agencies, and everyone has one within them.
- Pay attention to what color code you are in and react accordingly.
- Stay A.W.A.R.E.—be Alert, Watch, Assess, Respond, and Escape if needed.

CHAPTER 3

THE A.W.A.R.E. FORMULA

Let's say that Bri, Lili's roommate, has her parents' credit card and is free to use it anytime. When it comes time for Christmas shopping, she wants to impress her family and friends with some amazing gifts, so she heads for the mall on the evening before Christmas Eve. Generally, the week before Christmas, the malls extend their store hours to take advantage of those last-minute shoppers, and there are plenty of people still at the malls until closing time. First, Bri hits up the stores she likes and buys a few outfits and saves the best store for last: the Apple Store. Her gift list for all her family members is entirely Apple products. Hours later, the mall is closing, and she walks out with a lot of bags in her hand, all with the brand logos on the side. The biggest and brightest bag, the one that really stands out, is the white bag with the Apple logo on the side.

She walks out of the mall, toward the parking garage, and remembers she parked in the far corner, where she was forced to park because it was the last spot open when she arrived. At this point, Bri is feeling good about all of her gifts and can't wait to get home to wrap them. She is in her Yellow Color Code.

Then she notices a group of people standing near a car. She'll have to walk past them to get to her own car. As she gets closer to them, she realizes they look a bit shady, as they stare at all the goody bags Bri's holding. She starts to walk faster and realizes that they are following her. She starts to feel some fear and is soon in her Orange Color Code. She can hear them walking behind her. She starts walking even faster. I should mention that by this time, the parking garage is nearly empty. Bri is focused on hurrying as fast as possible to her car, which she knows she parked in the far corner of the lot. But now she's so flustered that she doesn't notice that her car isn't in the spot where she thought she parked it.

In the midst of her panicked state, she realizes she must have parked on the second level, not the third, and luckily there is a staircase nearby. She immediately turns into the stairwell and heads down the stairs as fast as she can, but after a few steps down, she realizes that no, she parked on the fourth level, not the second! She turns around to head back up the stairs and freezes because there in front of her are all of the shady people. Now she is in her Red Color Code because 90 percent of her safety, her A.W.A.R.E. mindset, has gone out the window. You, of course, will not do this, because you have read this book.

They may rob her now, or worse. If she could do something differently, take that night back and do it over again, what could she do to avoid getting into the 10 percent zone?

Here are some of the things Bri could have done. At the time she was walking out of the mall, she could have immediately turned around when she saw the group of people in the parking garage who looked a bit suspicious. She could have then headed back to the mall to find a security guard and request an escort to her car, or she could have waited to see if more people would appear, walking in the direction she was, so she could walk with them. She could have found a time to shop during daylight, when there are more crowds around, and of course, there is always the option of shopping online, purchasing an Apple gift card, and printing it out. She could have also brought her own shopping bag so no one would know what was in the bags.

If Bri had been educated in the A.W.A.R.E. formula and the five keys to managing personal safety—stay Alert, Watch for signs of trouble, Assess the situation, Respond appropriately, and Escape if necessary—she would not have gotten into this situation.

Think about that for a moment. If you were Bri, what could you have done to prepare yourself to not get into this situation?

Let's break each of these five strategies down:

Alert: In a situation like this, you would simply not go to a shopping mall late at night right before Christmas, and you certainly would not try to walk by a group of suspicious-looking people. You would either shop online, buy gift cards, shop during the day, or go get security the moment you noticed potential risk. Any of these would allow you to avoid the situation altogether. This way, you would avoid getting mugged.

Watch: Keep your eyes open. Later in the book, we will discuss how police officers and other law enforcement keep an eye on everything in their surroundings all the time. You can be this way too. Just focus on what's going on around you. Don't get pulled into your cell phone so much that you miss the real world unfolding around you.

Assess: Take a look at what's around you. Going back to the Thanksgiving grocery store incident with my sister, there were a lot of people in the store and only one crazy person. How likely was it that he would hurt anyone? It's hard to say, since someone or something may have triggered his already activated emotional state. Most likely, he was out of his mind, possibly drunk, or just emotionally distraught. You should use caution and, at the same time, assess what's going on around you to decide on the best response. Now, in Bri's case, how likely was it that she would get mugged in that parking garage? Not extremely surprising that this happened to her, is it? She made some questionable decisions and got herself into a situation. She was not watching, and when she did notice something, she did not assess it for danger.

Respond: After you have made an assessment, sometimes you will not need to respond to the situation. However, you should always take some kind of action or initiate some kind of response to any potentially risky person, place, or situation. Sometimes this just means walking in another direction to put some distance between yourself and the situation. Other times it means calling 911 and getting out of there. You may need to yell for help or go find another person. Once you're parked in a parking garage late at night, you should know that there is a potential situation that could happen and that you may need to respond to it. There is no shortage of thieves in parking garages looking for people with shopping bags they can rob or cars they can break into. If you sense possible danger, then respond. Take the proper steps to keep anything from happening to you or your belongings.

Escape: This is the last step and the most important, as it will determine your personal safety success.

These five pieces make up the A.W.A.R.E. mindset. For

example, you need to be alert and watch what's going on around you to respond to a risky situation. Even if you plan ahead to reduce the risk when you get somewhere, you still have to be A.W.A.R.E. once you get there.

In Bri's case, since she was already there at the mall with her packages, the minute she saw the people in the garage between her and her car, she should have turned around and gone to find a mall security guard. That would have been a smart response.

Imagine if it were even worse. What if Bri was not only walking into a parking garage alone late at night with high-end shopping bags in her hand but also talking to one of her friends on her phone? What if she wasn't aware of her surroundings and didn't even notice the group of people in the parking garage?

If you're on your phone when you're out in public like that, it's impossible to be fully aware. It can be too late before you even notice there is a risk ahead of you.

Plan ahead. If you do decide that you're going to walk through a parking garage late at night, don't be on your phone. Stay A.W.A.R.E. of your surroundings and stay in your Yellow Color Code for the entire time you are out shopping. Risk reduction begins before you even leave the house. Think through and plan out how you're going to stay safe when you leave your home, dorm, or apartment. However, if you can avoid walking to your car alone in a parking garage at night, then avoid it! That is common sense.

Personal safety comes down to this handful of five basic strategies. It starts with you reducing the possibility of a crime through planning, and once out, remaining in a state of alertness to your surroundings. You watch and assess, and you are then able to respond to any possible dangerous situations and escape if needed so you don't become a victim.

Think twice about what you are doing. Don't just non-chalantly assume you will always be fine. Even when you understand all the principles in this book, you will still need to stay A.W.A.R.E. and be on alert to protect your personal safety. However, if you continue to use the A.W.A.R.E. method in your daily life, it will become second nature. Right now, in fact, I'm writing this paragraph at my car dealership, waiting for my new tires to get put on. I'm stuck here for three hours! I arrived at 7:30 a.m. and was the first person in the waiting room. I found a smart spot to set up my laptop, put on my noise-canceling earbuds, and powered it up. I made sure I was in a good location in the waiting room and could see all of my surroundings. I took a look around to note the exits and any areas of vulnerability. To me, this is second nature. In your case, it's probably not yet embedded into your everyday thinking process, but it will be soon, once you start using the five steps of A.W.A.R.E.

Here are some basic dos and don'ts for staying A.W.A.R.E.:

- It's not just a cliché saying; there is truly strength in numbers, so bring a friend whenever you can.
- Don't go to an ATM at night.
- Be aware when going into elevators.
- Don't kid yourself; there are people out there who are committing crimes every day, and you need to watch out for them.
- Be informed, and don't take chances. Think: better safe than sorry.

By reading this book, you're educating yourself. In the future, you'll avoid suspicious situations.

If you see a questionable person, or several of them,

between you and where you are going, turn around and avoid them. Ask for help from someone else if you need to. You'll be in your Orange Color Code, but at least you can avoid getting into your Red Color Code and having to fight for your life.

RISKY PEOPLE

We can't talk about personal safety without talking about risky people. Bri had no trouble recognizing that the people in the garage looked risky. But this is the tricky part because, often, other people do not give you reliable visible clues about themselves. You often can't tell by just looking at someone whether they are the nicest person on earth or a dangerous criminal. You only have their actions to consider and, if it's available, any information you have about their background. You can tell when you might be going into a risky place or about to encounter a risky circumstance. You can feel those; they're intuitive. Those are easy to recognize. But when you are out of the nest and in the wild of the real world, you're going to encounter risky people, and it's not always so clear who is safe and who is not. People will scam you, or they will steal your money or your belongings.

You never really know someone until you've been around them for a long time. And sometimes, even if you have been around them for a long time, you may not really know them.

Use caution when using a rideshare app. Rideshare drivers are not always what they seem and have been known to do terrible things, like offer someone a water bottle that appears to be sealed but that actually has Rohypnol in it. A YouTube video recently showed a young girl explaining that her friend had just had this happen to her in an Uber Black in Los Angeles. The crime prevention tips offered in the video include calling the rideshare from indoors so that you're not standing outside longer than you need to, always checking the driver's name and license plate against what the app tells you, and getting out of the car immediately if you sense something is not quite right. Don't take water or food or anything like that from a driver.

One time when I was working at a university during a summer program, kids from all over the country were staying in the dorms for a couple of weeks for a college prep camp. Beautiful million-dollar homes line the top of the hill near the campus. Two young people from the camp found that one of these homes was not occupied, and they broke into it. They stayed at the house and took it over, ate the food, sprawled out on the couches, and watched the big-screen TV. They found the keys to the owner's Mercedes and took it for a joyride, even driving it to campus, as if it were their own car. They checked in at the dorm every day, just often enough to make it seem like they were staying in their rooms and attending the program, but then they would drive the car back to the house. When the owners returned from their international trip, they realized that strangers had been living in their house and their Mercedes was gone!

The point for college students (and any young people just out of the nest) to remember is that you may feel like you're in a safe environment on campus, but there is always the potential that someone you meet is not trustworthy. This is why it is crucial to be A.W.A.R.E., even when it comes to people you hang out with, and to be protective of your personal safety and your property, no matter what.

COMMON SENSE IS NOT COMMON ENOUGH

Use common sense. I like to say that, unfortunately, common sense isn't as common as it used to be. Know that people will sometimes pull the wool over your eyes, and they will not always mean everything they say. That's just common sense.

In the dorms, don't be afraid to make friends with everyone you meet. Many of the people you will meet will be your friends for your entire time in college and beyond. I truly believe that like attracts like, and in time, you will be able to determine who best fits in your circle of trust and who does not.

However, you will always need to stay aware of the fact that you can't trust everyone the minute you meet them. Pay attention to what people do and say, and be a good judge of character. Someone may start the fall semester in August acting reliably and seem completely trustworthy, but people can change. They can become influenced by peer pressure and start doing things they know they shouldn't be doing.

This goes back to you becoming a small fish in a big ocean of other people. The people around you don't know you, and you don't know them. You might feel pressured to make an impression, to prove to other people from all over the country and world that you belong and fit in. At the same time, they will be doing the same thing—trying to prove themselves in this new environment.

Many dorms have three or four roommates in a suite. Most have at least two roommates. The other people you're living with now may have grown up in a community where nobody needed to lock their front doors. Maybe they didn't have much crime in their town and never felt the need to protect their personal safety. But now they do. Their habit of not locking doors might put you in danger. It's up to you to keep your belongings and your valuables safe.

PREPARING FOR A TRIP

Recently, I attended a five-day conference in another state, and I had to do quite a bit of planning and preparation. The whole week before the trip, I was very preoccupied with getting ready and thinking about what to pack. How would I get to and from the airport? What time of day would I arrive at the conference hotel venue, and how could I make sure I arrived there during the day and not at night? How far was it from the airport to the hotel? What was the weather going to be like in this city I'd never been to?

You can think about the A.W.A.R.E. mindset, when you're out of the nest and in the wild of the real world, as similar to packing for a trip. When you're going on a trip, you have to know what the weather is going to be like, how long you're going to be there, how you'll get there and back, what you'll be doing when you're there, and what the people and culture, customs, and potential risks are. Then you can make all the appropriate plans and reservations and arrangements. You'll know what to wear and what you should and shouldn't do when you are there.

When you go off to college, you have to prepare in much the same way. You have to decide what to bring, you have to know when to be where, and you hopefully have some support in place with friends or family to help you through any initial homesickness. Once you're there and settled in, things really get busy, and there are so many things you have to plan and prepare for: making sure you aren't going to be left alone at a party, keeping your phone charged, getting safe rides, and knowing where you're going and who you are going with.

You'll constantly be assessing whether this or that situation sounds safe and would be a smart thing to do. As you gather more information over time, you should be frequently assessing whether the people you are hanging out with are good and trustworthy and safe. Make sure you always have at least one person you trust going with you. This brings me to the concept of the buddy system.

THE PROMISE OF BUDDIES

One of the best ways to put risk reduction into place is by leaning into the buddy system. When you're utilizing the buddy system, before you go out, you make sure you have someone to go with. You make a promise to that person that you will not leave them and they will not leave you. You cannot break that promise.

Risky situations are real, so be informed about how you can avoid being put at risk. For instance, you may be at a party; you've got a buddy nearby, and everything is fine, and you're having a good time. Then, out of nowhere, there are loud noises of shouting and a fight. Maybe a couple of guys have gotten into an argument, and now they're brawling. This probably has nothing to do with you, but now you've got to grab your buddy and get out of there.

In Lili's case, she didn't use any of the strategies of the A.W.A.R.E. mindset. She didn't assess the situation. She didn't have time to plan or think about what she should and shouldn't do at a college party. She also didn't have recognition that there would be a risk in taking a drink she didn't see being made and that she could get roofied when the guy turned his back, and she certainly did not do what she should have to escape from being raped, because by that point, she couldn't.

She could have asked to make her own drink, or she could have watched what he was doing carefully by moving in closer.

In this day and age, you have to be careful. But she was young, she had just left the nest, and she was at a party with a lot of good-looking guys. She's petite and attractive and was just trying to have a good time, listening to the music and checking people out. That's all fine, but it doesn't mean she should stop being A.W.A.R.E. of any potential risks.

Lili was quite impressed by all the good-looking people at this party. She'd never pictured herself being at a party like this. But for Bri, it was nothing. It was just another party. She's a rich socialite who goes out with guys and drinks all the time. She's oblivious to the dangers in her own way, as we saw at the beginning of this chapter.

These five parts of the A.W.A.R.E. formula—Alert, Watch, Assess, Respond, and Escape—are the pillars that will hold up the house of your personal safety. Armed with all five, you will greatly enhance your chances of never being a victim of a crime.

If Bri had used even just one of these strategies, such as recognizing danger, she would have realized she was entering a potentially bad situation in that parking garage. Instead, she just plowed ahead to her car, when she could have avoided the mugging and the loss of her Christmas gifts for her family.

There are many plans and decisions you can make before you ever set out when leaving your home, whether it be to go to a party, shopping mall, concert, or even the drive-through. These preparations and precautions will help you avoid risk and victimization by removing the opportunities you may be giving a criminal unknowingly. In the next chapter, we will take a deeper look at the Victim Pyramid and how to think in terms of removing the opportunity for a crime to happen in the first place.

CHAPTER 3: STAY A.W.A.R.E. TAKEAWAYS

- Plan your outings, especially when going alone or after dark.
- Practice the A.W.A.R.E. mindset in your daily routine.
- When walking in public places or sitting in a public place, stay off your phone and be aware of your surroundings.

CHAPTER 4

THE VICTIM PYRAMID

A couple of months after Lili learned she was pregnant, she dropped out of school. Bri pulled some strings, based on her legacy status, to arrange for her friend Sara to move in. Sara had joined the same sorority Bri was in, and they'd become best friends. Sara liked going out, drinking, and boys; she lived a similar lifestyle to Bri, and they had a lot in common, although she was more cautious and safety-oriented than Bri. Pretty soon, the two of them started having small gatherings in their dorm room.

Bri and Sara's dorm room was one of a few different rooms in the building that hosted parties on any given night of the week. Sara had brought a Cuisinart blender to school from home, and the two of them soon became known for their margaritas and piña coladas. They were careful not to get caught by their resident assistant (RA), and they kept the noise level down, but their parties occasionally got loud, and they were reprimanded a few times. One night, a crowd of kids was in the room. Most of them were from the sorority that Bri and Sara belonged to, but a couple of them were girls Bri and Sara had never seen before. They didn't think much of it, though, since these two girls brought beer and they seemed nice and fun. But the next day, Bri opened up her bedside table drawer and realized that the gold-and-diamond cross necklace her grandmother had given her was gone. She had been wearing it just the day before and thought she remembered putting it away in the drawer the night before—or did she leave it on top of her dresser? She panicked—that necklace had been handed down in her family for generations.

"Hey, Sara," Bri asked. "Have you seen my diamond cross necklace?"

"No, the last time I saw it, you were wearing it. Where did you leave it?" Sara said.

"I'm not sure, but I think I put it in my jewelry box..." She pointed to a see-through glass and metal box that clearly held a lot of jewelry and had no lock.

"Does that thing even lock?" Sara asked.

Bri looked at her with a guilty expression.

Sara rolled her eyes. "Really, Bri? You might as well just hand it over to someone if you're going to leave your stuff lying around like that. You can't be so trusting of people—especially if strangers are coming into our dorm."

Bri knew Sara was right, but she got defensive for a minute. "Well, at least I'm not walking around paranoid all the time," Bri threw back at her.

Sara gave her a bewildered look. "What about those girls last night? Do you know who they came with?" Sara asked.

Bri shook her head. "No. I thought you knew them."

They looked at each other, realizing that the girls did not look familiar at all and could have been thieves. Bri looked through her jewelry box again and gasped. "Oh my God. My pearl earrings are gone too!"

The girls realized they'd been robbed, and there was no way to know who did it.

It was no secret that Bri came from a wealthy family, but it had never occurred to her that if they were going to have people in their room, they needed to secure their valuables in a safe place. Sara's parents both worked in medicine, so they were well-off, too, but because of their careers, they were especially strict about personal safety. Her mom was an ICU nurse, and her dad had seen it all in the ER. Sara had heard it all growing up.

But Bri wasn't used to thinking about how to keep her things safe. Her town was safe, and her parents lived a quiet life. She didn't understand the concept of the Victim Pyramid, which is all about not allowing anyone to make you a victim. She'd never needed to do that back home, or even in the dorm when she lived with Lili, who was as trustworthy as they come.

THE VICTIM PYRAMID

The Victim Pyramid is a way of thinking about crime prevention and personal safety that focuses on opportunity. If you think of a crime as a triangular shape, like a pyramid, on one side of the pyramid is the victim of the crime, you, and on the other side of the pyramid is the perpetrator of the crime, the assailant. The *foundation* of the pyramid is the opportunity that the victim has given to the perpetrator. In R.A.D. classes, we tell students to "remove the foundation of opportunity." When you do this, the Victim Pyramid crumbles and the crime doesn't happen.

THE VICTIM PYRAMID

There's nothing complex about this; it's really quite simple. Remove the foundation of the pyramid—the opportunity for a crime to happen—and you won't become a victim.

It's common sense, but there are several specific actions you can take when it comes to removing the factor of opportunity from the victim equation.

- Stay alert. You need to have an A.W.A.R.E. mindset about your surroundings to remove the foundation of opportunity.
- Remember that bad things can happen, and they can happen to you if you're allowing others to prey on you.
- Trust your instincts. Your gut often knows before your brain that there's something not right in your surroundings. Don't ignore that message. Listen to it and take appropriate action.
- Consider whether something you are doing will give someone else the opportunity to commit a crime.

Remember, the goal is to prevent yourself from becoming a victim.

In our handbook and manual for Rape Aggression Defense (R.A.D.) Systems, they include this quote:

"The only confrontation you are guaranteed to survive every time is the one you are never involved in."

By removing the foundation of the pyramid—the opportunity—it's much less likely that you'll be a victim of a crime.

Some years ago, I was working in crime prevention for the Hayward Police Department when a person called me to report a theft from their car. The man called me, asking for extra patrolling in his neighborhood, which was a nice neighborhood, and I asked him why he was requesting this. He told me that his mother's car had just been broken into. It was her birthday, he told me, and she had driven a long way to visit him. She'd opened her gifts during the birthday celebration and then put the gifts in her car outside. Later, she decided to spend the night. Her son went out and covered his mother's gifts with his leather jacket, thinking that would hide them, but he didn't cover the leather jacket, so the next morning the car was broken into, and all of his mom's gifts were stolen.

I asked him, "Where did you leave the presents?"

He said, "They were in the front seat of the car. I went out and covered them with my leather jacket to hide them."

I thought to myself, *Are you fricken kidding me, dude?*

At that point, I realized that this person had given too much opportunity to the criminal who had robbed him. The burglar only saw the leather jacket and, to his surprise, got so much more than just a nice leather jacket.

A similar thing happened near the Oakland airport. A couple flew in and rented a car, but someone was watching them at the rental car center and followed them. They drove a few towns over to Hayward, and they stopped at a chain restaurant—an Applebee's or similar—just off the freeway. They went inside to eat, and when they came back out, the rental car had been broken into. Their luggage and backpacks and everything else they'd left in the car was gone. Inside one of the backpacks was an engagement ring the man was going to give his girlfriend when they reached their destination in Monterey.

I learned about this the next morning, reading the watch commander's log, like I do every morning.

This man's plan to propose was completely ruined because he gave a thief the opportunity to rob them. If you are carrying something important around, keep it with you. My brother almost did something similar. He was getting ready to propose to his girlfriend, who is now his wife. They were flying to New York, where he planned to propose to her at the top of the Empire State Building. He showed me the ring, and I told him the story of the couple who flew into Oakland.

I said, "Do me a favor: keep the ring on your person somewhere so you'll know it's safe. Don't put it in your luggage, because it could get lost forever." It was a very expensive and custom-made ring, so I was pretty sure he did not want to lose it. He said he was going to put it in his backpack and bring it on the plane. I urged him to keep it actually on him. I said, "Bring the ring box and put it in there if you can, but if not, then just put the ring in your pocket if the box is too big." Sure enough, he ended up having to check in his luggage and his backpack because they needed to lighten up the cabin. And guess what? His luggage and backpack never made it to JFK Airport. Luckily, my brother listened to me and still had the ring!

In these kinds of cases, the only way to remove the opportunity is to keep your valuables with you—directly on you. In law enforcement, we are taught that you have to secure your belongings first.

It doesn't matter what it is; if it's valuable to you, don't leave it in your car. The same goes for places on campus, like the library, the food hall, a coffee shop, or even a gym locker. If you're not on campus, the rule still applies for restaurants, parks, beaches, and any public places.

The Victim Pyramid applies to other crimes, too, not just theft. If you don't want to be a victim of sexual assault while on a first date, don't go out alone with him, and stay in public places. Even if you know him from class or through a mutual friend, don't put yourself in a situation where you're alone with someone you barely know. Definitely don't go to his room or apartment, or anything like that, unless you are completely familiar and comfortable with that person and know him and his circle of friends well.

Whenever you can, bring a friend and use the buddy system, and never break the promise—you stick together. It works both ways—you have to stick with them and they stick with you. It doesn't matter if you and your friend are both in the same class with this guy and one of you leaves the other one with him. That's not your promise to each other. You can't leave each other. You don't abandon the ship. You have to keep the promise.

Many people don't realize that if you just take away the opportunity, you will most likely not be a victim. The crime is far less likely to happen, no matter how high the crime rate is around you or how expensive your valuables are.

Without the sun, trees don't grow. It's a fundamental law of nature that if you take away the opportunity for a crime to happen, it won't happen.

REMOVABLE OPPORTUNITIES

There are three main types of sexual assault that we see out in the world, and they each come with different ways for you to remove the opportunity and not become a victim.

The first and worst-case scenario is a serial rapist/killer who is deranged and looking for the opportunity to rape and kill women that he doesn't know. These despicable criminals will often prey on women in certain places where there are a lot of females. To avoid this type of sexual assault, you need to remove the opportunity by never being in a place where you might be vulnerable to a madman like that.

If you think about Ted Bundy, he was in this severe category of rapist. He was good-looking and had a horrific upbringing. He would help women and then entrap them, then enjoy seeing them suffer during the rape, then kill them. As a child, his mother made him do very strange things, and he grew up to be a psychopath. Unfortunately, there are still a lot of psychopaths out on the streets.

With a Ted Bundy situation, all you have to rely on to remove the opportunity are your decisions about where you go and who you go there with, your awareness of your surroundings once you're there, and your gut instincts, which might sense that something is off before your brain realizes it. I'm not trying to scare you, but we have to get real here. You are a young adult heading out into the real world, and you're going to meet a lot of new people, so it's beneficial for you to have this information and awareness, even if it is uncomfortable to think about.

To remove the foundation of opportunity for this type of crime to happen, you need to stay aware. Wherever you are, if you think or feel that there is even the slightest possibility for something horrible to happen, you should leave immediately. If a stranger offers to help you with something, do not accept that offer.

The second type of sexual assault you must be aware of is what is commonly known as "date" rape, a form of acquaintance rape, but is actually just "rape" that stems from two people who have been in a relationship, platonically or sexually.

Rape between people who know each other is all too common. The National Institute of Justice states, "About 85 to 90 percent of sexual assaults reported by college women are perpetrated by someone known to the victim; about half occur on a date."[1]

In other words, it's more likely you'd be a victim of rape by someone you know and who knows you than by a stranger.

A Medical News Today article also states that most rapes on college campuses occur between a man and a woman who

---

1   National Institute of Justice, "Most Victims Know Their Attacker," September 30, 2008, https://nij.ojp.gov/topics/articles/most-victims-know-their-attacker.

already know each other.[2] This article also asserts that the use of "date rape" drugs is on the rise. The drugs make it difficult for their victims to say no. Other drugs can physically weaken a victim, making it harder for them to fight the assailant off; they can knock them unconscious and even just lower the victim's inhibitions so they go along with an act they would not agree to if they were sober.

Any drug that changes your state of mind can be used during a sexual assault. Some of the more common ones include alcohol, marijuana, Xanax or a similar anti-anxiety medication, and ketamine.

For this type of sexual assault, you can remove the opportunity to become a victim by taking stock of the people you know and the people you meet and staying alert, watching for any signs that they may have criminal intentions. And of course, you can never accept a drink you did not make or pour, and you can cover your drink securely if you're walking away from it.

It's sad, but many young men don't realize that forcing themselves on a girl they know constitutes rape. Someone you know might not realize that "no means no," but that doesn't make them any less of a sexual predator if they force you to have sex with them against your will. On most college campuses, the campus police actually don't deal with with too many sexual assault cases between people who know each other because more often than not, they are never reported.

The takeaway here for a teen or young adult leaving the nest is this: don't assume that just because you know someone, or you know someone who knows them, that they're safe.

---

2   Zawn Villines, "What You Should Know About Date Rape Drugs," Medical News Today, updated May 2, 2025, https://www.medicalnewstoday.com/articles/320409.

Even if you know them, you still need to be careful because every so often, someone you think you know well may have a side to them that is not what you'd expect.

Another type of sexual assault situation does not involve knowing someone, and the crime does not involve murder. These are the kinds of rapes that were reported the most at the university. Predators would come onto campus looking for young girls; find an opportunity, such as a private area or a dark time of day with few people around; and knock out the victim, rape them, and leave them there. Unfortunately, we have seen too many of these. They are almost always reported right away, and so they are the most typical experiences law enforcement sees on campuses.

STAY WITH YOUR BUDDY

When we worked with younger kids in our r.a.d.KIDS classes, we used a simulation called Sight, Sound, Distance to demonstrate how far children should stray away from their parents in a store, playground, or any public place. The child has to be able to see and hear their parents, and the parents have to be able to see and hear the child. The child also needs to be close enough to their parents to be able to run to them before they are abducted. The kids will estimate this distance themselves, and we will let them know if that distance is too far away from their parents or other adults to be considered safe. Usually the child estimates a distance that is too far away from their parents. We correct the distance for them so they can see and feel for themselves how far they should stray.

Had Lili been more aware and proactive at the party, she might have said to Bri, "You will know a lot of people at this party, and I won't, so let's keep an eye out for each other."

The key here is the buddy system. Check in with your buddy from time to time to make sure they are okay, and if you see your buddy being forced to use a beer bong or being harassed by other partygoers to take shots, then you can intervene and take your buddy away. To remove the opportunity, of course, Lili could have also not accepted the drink. She could have planned the evening, anticipating that Bri would be a social butterfly at the party, and found a third person to go with them. If that didn't work, she could have stuck with Bri or at least looked for her when she disappeared. At least, she could have grabbed a sealed bottle of water or a can of soda and drank that, just to be safe. Any of these actions could have removed the opportunity for her to become a victim of a crime.

REMOVE THE FOUNDATION OF OPPORTUNITY FOR THEFT

Rape isn't the only type of crime we are concerned with in this book, however. Other types of crimes, such as theft and physical assault, can still be quite serious. Many of the same rules apply when you're trying to remove the opportunity to be a victim.

If you want to prevent theft in your dorm room, I suggest that everyone have a routine, a system of sorts, where things such as expensive watches or tech tools get placed in a secure area. Maybe you have a container for those things under your bed or in your closet. It's important to keep things either hidden or secured. You can also buy a small personal safe for around forty dollars. Especially when it comes to your cash, jewelry, high-end electronics, and other valuables, it's worth it to protect yourself from theft.

When I was a student at Hayward, my husband, whom

I met there, was paired with a roommate who was from his hometown. They grew up just a small city away from each other and knew each other. They figured they could travel home together if they wanted. But the bonus to that type of roommate is that there is a common ground and common background. Often, however, incoming freshmen want to experience all of the diversity that college has to offer as well. Part of the excitement is getting to know people from all over. In this case, you can look for people you have common interests with and who share your values. Use the college or university's online roommate matching app or an app such as BeRoomie or Roomsurf.

Distractions are another consideration when it comes to theft. When you are launching from your home to the bigger world, your life will be filled with distractions no matter where you end up. Your social life and your academic or work life will pull you in a million different directions. Try to keep your safety at the front of your mind and not lose yourself in all the activities and learning that you're constantly exposed to.

WHAT WE ARE ACTUALLY REMOVING

Often in my presentations at high schools and colleges, students will ask me what they have to get rid of to get rid of the opportunity. Do you have to get rid of yourself, meaning not going anywhere that could be risky? That way, the assailant is going to just find another victim. But a lot of people don't realize that you can be in a somewhat risky situation and still not be a victim. The key is to not give them a reason to victimize you. Many people don't realize that if a criminal doesn't have a reason to rob you, they won't rob you. You can't give them the reason; you have to take it away. One example is the inside of your car. You should never have valuables of any kind visible inside your locked vehicle, because windows are smashed and doors are jimmied almost every minute somewhere in this country. It's easy money for those criminals. Appearing confident is another example. Carry yourself with poise and purpose. Don't walk around looking unaware of your surroundings. Just act cool, like you own the place. Be smooth and in control. Your confident vibe will come off to potential criminals as intimidating and not worth the effort.

Opportunity is (almost) everything. When he was about thirteen or fourteen, my son got an expensive bicycle for his birthday and was riding around town with it. For some reason, the bike he chose was bright metallic green. I thought it was hideous, but my son loved it. He had gone through my r.a.d.KIDS class, and the Victim Pyramid had been instilled in him from an early age. He knew the motto: "Remove the foundation of opportunity to prevent the crime." One afternoon, I happened to be driving through town and drove by a local Taco Bell where all the kids always hung out. As I drove by, I couldn't help but notice a bright metallic green bike leaning up against the wall near the entrance of the Taco Bell. I couldn't imagine another kid in our town wanting to get a hideous bright metallic green bike like my son's, so I pulled over to the side of the street and called his cell phone. I asked him where he was.

"Taco Bell," he said.

"Where's your bike?" I asked.

"Outside."

"Why?"

"Mom, it's fine. We will run out and stop anyone who tries to steal our bikes."

"Really? You and your cousin will stop them?"

My son was about eighty pounds (soaking wet, that is), and his cousin was even younger and smaller. I said, "Do you remember the thing you learned about the Victim Pyramid in r.a.d.KIDS?"

"Yes, I remember," he said.

"Your bikes are very expensive, and all it takes is some big, burly father whose son would love a bike like that to pull up to the curb and throw both of those bikes in the back of his truck and take off. The freeway is only a block away!"

There was silence as he thought.

"Hold on, Mom."

A few seconds later, I looked over at the Taco Bell and saw him and his cousin come out and take their bikes and bring them inside the restaurant. Opportunity removed. No crime of opportunity.

After you've read this book, hopefully this way of thinking ahead to prevent crime will come more naturally to you. I've been working in this field for twenty-five years, so it's become second nature to me. I hope that it will become second nature to you, too, after you practice it for a while.

My goal is to make you change your paradigm when it comes to your safety. When you finish this book, you'll have learned something that will change your way of thinking when it comes to your safety. You'll understand that personal safety isn't just random good or bad luck; your level of awareness can make a huge difference in how likely you are to become a victim of a crime.

You should always be thinking, *If I take away the opportunity, I will not be a victim of a crime.* I tell people all the time to have a routine for where they put their valuables, for the same reason that I always put my keys, purse, or backpack in the same place—that way, I don't have to think about it. So, even if you come home late, instead of just putting something down in any old place, have a special place to put your important things, hidden away or secured, so you don't even have to think about it. You will do it automatically. If Bri had created a special and secure place for her grandmother's heirloom necklace and had developed a habit of always keeping it there, it most likely would not have been stolen. She would have hidden it away and removed the opportunity for someone to steal it, no matter how tired she was the night before.

The purpose of this book is to give you information and knowledge so you can keep yourself safe and make good choices now that you have or will be leaving the nest and going into the wild. However, if you find yourself outside of 90 percent of your safety and into your 10 percent, which is in your Red Color Code, you will have to defend yourself. In the next chapter, we'll break down strategies for using your personal weapons—certain parts of your body—to fend off an assailant and escape to safety.

CHAPTER 4: STAY A.W.A.R.E. TAKEAWAYS

- Remove the foundation of opportunity to prevent the crime.
- Don't leave your valuables out in plain sight.
- Use the buddy system.

THE OTHER 10 PERCENT

Sara, Bri's new roommate, attended a self-defense class in high school and learned many of the concepts and defensive techniques in this book. By the time she arrived on campus, she was more aware than most.

One night, she was walking home from a party, by herself, to her dorm room. She knew better than to walk home alone, but she had ended up staying at the party later than Bri, and there had been no one else she felt comfortable asking to walk her back. The walk would be well lit and out in the open, except for one narrow and dimly lit walkway she had to get through. She was scurrying through that narrow walkway when a man suddenly appeared out of the darkness and moved toward her. Before she knew it, he had grabbed her left wrist and was trying to hold her there. She immediately went into her Red Color Code and thought through her options with lightning speed.

She turned to face her assailant and immediately established her base (balanced herself), made a fist with her right hand, lifted her arm, and planted a "hammer fist" onto the assailant's forearm that was holding her as she loudly yelled "NO!" He immediately let go, and as she was trying to break free, he grabbed her from behind, like a bear hug, to control her. Sara used her voice and yelled, "Help me! Someone help me!" With the assailant's tight grip around her, she was able to establish her base (gain control of her balance) and, in one smooth motion, planted a heel strike to his groin and, with the same leg, took her wedge heel and scraped his shin and heel-stomped the top of his toes. Sara disengaged and evaluated her assailant and saw that he was in excruciating pain; then she escaped. Sara ran to a safe place and called the police.

Ninety percent of our personal safety depends on our ability to stay A.W.A.R.E., but there are times when even that is not enough. In these times, we have to use our other 10 percent. The other 10 percent entails using our personal weapons to defend ourselves. From the top down, our personal weapons include our forehead, back of head, hands (fists), elbows, knees, and feet.

During my time as a self-defense instructor for R.A.D. Systems, we spent many hours teaching students how to use their personal weapons, which are certain body parts we all have that can seriously hurt an attacker regardless of whether they are bigger than their victim or not.

The full R.A.D. Systems training for personal safety is a unique and valuable course, and I encourage everyone to take it. The twelve hours of self-defense training is broken down into three parts:

1. Lecture and discussion on awareness, risk reduction, the Victim Pyramid, and the Color Code of Awareness (three to four hours*). This is your 90 percent.

2. Strikes, blocks, kicks, escape moves, and learning physical techniques with pads (six to seven hours*). This is the intro to the 10 percent of defending yourself.
3. Simulation of fighting off an attack with one to five assailants (with safety pads; one to three hours*). This is your 10 percent!

*These times will vary depending on the size of the class.

When I started to teach personal safety on my own, I was primarily visiting college campuses to speak. I needed a ninety-minute version of the twelve-hour course to present the basic ideas of personal safety and the A.W.A.R.E. concepts to students. I narrowed the course content down to just the 90 percent because the hope is that if you fully understand the 90 percent of your personal safety and always utilize the A.W.A.R.E. method, you'll most likely never find yourself in a situation that requires you to use the other 10 percent.

However, there is always the possibility that all of the elements of the A.W.A.R.E. method will not be enough, and you'll be forced to fight back. This chapter is here to help you gain some basic knowledge about the most effective self-defense tool you'll have in those cases: your personal weapons.

First, I want to explain that there are several differences between martial arts and what I teach, which is self-defense. You can certainly use martial arts to protect yourself, and it is great for that. But what I teach is how to use your own awareness, information, and knowledge to avoid and escape victimization and then, only if necessary, how to use your own personal weapons to defend yourself and escape the situation.

The concept of using your personal weapons is not taught to people enough, in my opinion. It's truly amazing what some of our own body parts can do to disable an attacker. Your hands alone can be used as four different types of weapons.

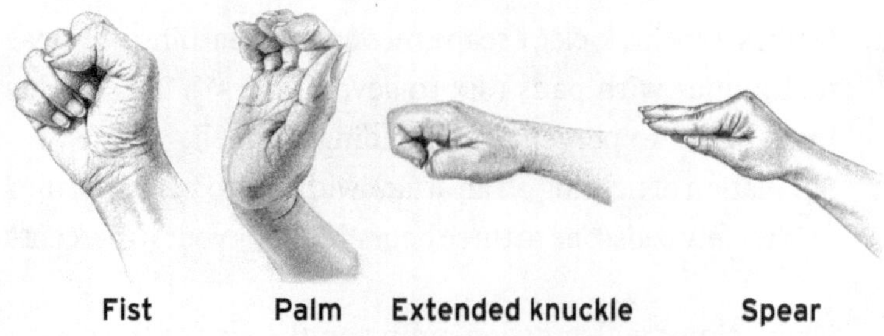

You can make a fist or flatten your hand so that your fingers are like spears, capable of stabbing someone in the eyes, or the base of the palm of your hand can be used to break someone's nose, or the extended knuckle pose can be used to punch a vulnerable area on their body, such as the chin or throat.

Other personal weapons we will discuss include your elbows, forehead, back of the head, knees, and feet. One of the most vital of your personal weapons is your voice. If you can yell for help, you should always do so. Even just yelling loudly at the assailant, like "Stop! Leave me alone! Get your f*cking hands off me!" is very effective in startling them enough that they will leave you alone, and also other people will hear you.

Your *personal weapons* are great tools, but you have to know how to use them effectively to be successful; identifying your attacker's *vulnerable locations* is key to this self-defense strategy. Your knee and fist, for instance, can temporarily paralyze an assailant if you use them to forcefully strike up into their groin.

There are ten vulnerable locations on an assailant, from top to bottom: eyes, nose, chin, throat, fingers, forearms, torso, groin, shins, and feet. The tops of their feet (toes), shins, forearms, fingers, torso, and chin are moderately vulnerable locations on an assailant but still effective if those areas are targeted by your personal weapons effectively. The eyes, nose, and groin are considered more extreme and can cause more damage to the assailant when you use your personal weapons correctly. Determining the appropriate defensive move is important; you need to assess whether the danger is moderate or extreme. You don't want to use extreme force in a moderate situation; otherwise, you might be committing assault. Neither do you want to use a moderate move in an extremely dangerous situation, because obviously that could lead to you losing the fight. That is not what we want to happen. The whole point of this book is to help you learn to defend yourself from becoming a victim, and if it comes down to a serious physical confrontation, you will need to defend yourself as if your life depends on it—because it may. Always remember that the goal is to *escape*!

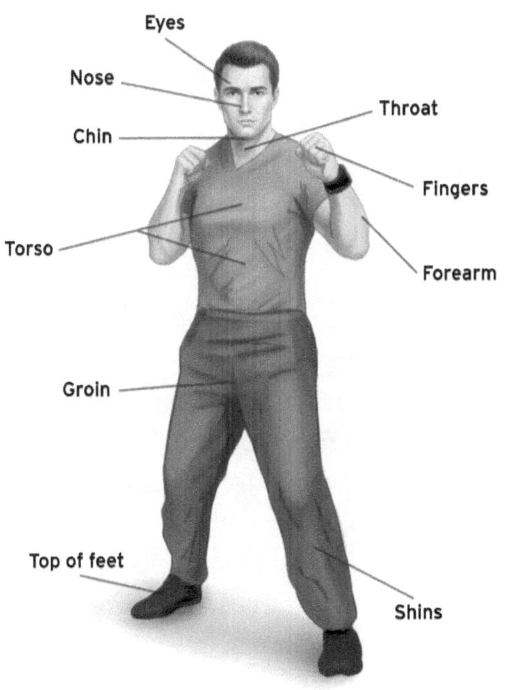

While most of your personal weapons are your own body parts, the other 10 percent sometimes includes using a nearby object as well. If someone is dragging you across a room, you can grab a lamp and hit them in the back of the head. If someone has broken into your house or apartment and is trying to sexually assault you, you can take the kitchen toaster or any small, heavy object to smash them in the face.

There are many other ways you can disable someone without anything but your own personal weapons.

You can do a lot of damage with these moves:

1. You can use your foot to kick or your knee to strike your assailant's groin area.
2. You can use your fingers as a spear to poke them in the eyes.
3. You can make a fist and hammer it down on their forearm so they will let go of your wrist or hit their nose with it.
4. You can take your elbow and give a strong elbow strike to the head, face, or torso.

This is only a short list of examples of moves you can make to disarm your attacker enough to escape and call for help. We will share many more in this chapter, and for even more resources, you can explore the Rape Aggression Defense Systems' techniques on your own.

It's important to clarify that some moves are not as effective at stopping them from continuing the attack as other moves. Biting, for instance, will only cause pain and possibly anger, while the massive force of your fist on their outstretched forearm can make them feel so much pain they'll think you broke their arm and be immobilized, at least for the few seconds you'll need to break free and escape.

The bones in a person's foot are very fragile and can easily be broken, which is extremely painful. If you stomp on someone with full force, you can smash their foot so badly that they won't be able to run after you. They might be able to hobble after you, but they might not even be able to manage that. Also remember that what you can do with your left foot or knee, you can always do with your right. Same with your fist strikes.

During a struggle, it is supremely important to keep your balance and focus on your plan of attack. Depending on what you can find around you to pick up and use, how will you knock this guy out? Will you be able to knock him out? If you can't knock him out, what other options do you have to immobilize him so you can quickly escape? What are all of the options available to you to win this fight? While your mind is swirling on these questions, your body should be focused on staying balanced so that you don't get thrown off balance or knocked to the ground.

When I share all the options of using personal weapons and identifying vulnerable locations with my students in my personal safety presentations, I tell them that this is just a teaser course. If you want to get empowered and learn 100 percent of self-defense and experience the full-fledged journey of acquiring skills in this area, you can find a self-defense class near you or go to the R.A.D. Systems website (https://www.rad-systems.com/) and find an in-person course where you can learn the physical portion of self-defense. It is a life-changing twelve-hour course, and you will want all your friends and family members to take the class. It is worth it. It was worth it for me!

SEVEN STRATEGIES OF SELF-DEFENSE

1. Establish a base—This is the idea of getting yourself into a defensive stance, one where you can strike and kick most easily.
2. Head butt
3. Hammer fist
4. Groin strike
5. Heel kick
6. Shin scrape
7. Heel stomp

If someone grabs your arm and tries to take your purse, let go of your purse. There's nothing in your purse that is more valuable than your own life, so let go of your purse and call the police, and be sure to be a good witness and give a good description. But if they are grabbing you and trying to take you away or drag you somewhere, you should start by verbalizing loudly, "Help! Somebody help me! Let go of me! Help!"

It's extremely important to first establish your base/balance, then take your fist and hit their forearm with your full force. This will usually cause them to let go. This way, you can escape. Their arm hurts, but they can still chase you. So then you need to escape as fast as possible, and you need to yell, "Help! Somebody help me! Stay back!" At least in this situation, you will have more options for self-defense than you did when he had you in his hold.

Learn as many of these techniques as possible so that you have a combination of options and can choose to do whatever is appropriate for the situation you're in. As mentioned at the beginning of this chapter, Sara used a combination of heel strike, shin scrape, and heel stomp in one motion. Along with knowing as many of these defensive moves as possible, you'll want to keep your personal weapons and knowledge of vulnerable areas on an assailant's body in mind. Starting with the top of your head, your personal weapons are:

Your forehead, the back of your head, your elbows, your hands (as fists, spears, palms, or extended knuckles), knees, and feet. Finally, you also have your voice to call out for help. You use these personal weapons to strike an assailant to break free or disarm or disable them. When you're using these personal weapons, you're directing the force at the assailant's vulnerable body parts: their eyes, nose, neck, groin, hands, and feet.

Severely vulnerable body parts include the eyes, the nose, and the groin, all of which can be debilitating. The eyes, in particular, are an effective choice if you can do it well. What is the impact of that going to be? If you blind them, of course, it's severe, but it's also severe on a couple of other levels. It's going to be painful and frightening for someone to have their eyes poked. Mentally, they are going to panic because they are suddenly unable to see, and then, obviously, the third level of impact on your target, the assailant, is that they won't be able to see you, which makes them highly impaired from continuing to attack you.

A strike to the nose is not necessarily lethal if you use the palm of your hand to strike it upward from beneath the nostrils; that's a myth. However, if you do this with enough force, you can break their nose, which will cause enough pain to at least temporarily disable them.

The third severely vulnerable body part is the groin. There are three ways to use this body part. You can kick it, punch it, or grab and seize, pulling down on the testicles. This causes great pain. Depending on your position and the position of your assailant, you would do whichever is easiest for you to do.

Moderately vulnerable body parts are the hands, forearms, neck, torso, shins, and feet. Striking any of these areas isn't likely to kill anyone or even stop them from hurting you. But it can still be effective in helping you escape, especially when used in combination with striking any other vulnerable areas you can reach.

Remember the color codes from Chapter 2? Those color codes are also important to keep in mind in the unfortunate event of an attack. When you're in your Yellow Color Code, you're relaxed and at ease, but you're still aware of your surroundings. You're keeping an eye out for anything out of the ordinary or suspicious. If you start to sense, even mildly, that there might be danger, you move into your Orange Color Code. You feel a physical sensation of fear, but you are still unsure, and your stress level rises a bit. Maybe your heart starts beating faster or your body tenses up. This means it's time to escape. Just leave—get out of the situation. If, for some reason, you cannot leave, you will need to fight for your life, and so you will need to be in your Red. You need to fight for your life. You escape at this point using whatever measures possible. Sometimes that can even mean mortally wounding someone.

The color codes also connect to the different defensive stances.

Imagine you are standing somewhere and your feet are spread about the width of your body, maybe a little wider. Your nondominant foot is slightly in front of the other one, and you're balanced in this position. You're in a relaxed but aware stance. You're in your Yellow Color Code and in a Cautious Contact Stance. If you see a bar fight breaking out right in front of you, then you respond by changing your stance.

Here are three stages of stances that correspond to the

three main color codes of awareness. When you're in your Yellow Color Code, you should take a Cautious Contact Stance. When something causes your internal awareness to elevate you to an Orange Color Code and you sense danger is near, you move into a Warning Contact Stance where both your arms are up in front of you, preparing for anything or anyone to come at you. And if you end up in that other 10 percent, your Red Color Code, you need to move into the Defensive Stance. This is where you are in a physical altercation and you are in survival mode.

Cautious contact   Warning contact   Defensive stance

AN EYE FOR AN EYE

We had an incident in one of our R.A.D. classes during the final portion of the class, which is called the simulation. We have a total of five assailants who wear the RedMan suit. Each student has to defend against all five assailants in three different scenarios. Each student has to fight every assailant to escape. If a student doesn't use any of the self-defense options taught to them, the assailant will not let go. Most of the students are so focused that they do exactly what they are taught. One time, the assailant was already down on the ground after a student had kneed him in the groin. The student was so fired up that she went over and kicked him in the head like a soccer ball. He wasn't expecting the student to return and wasn't prepared to take the blow to the head. He was hurt pretty badly and ended up having to retire from teaching. Self-defense simulation and real life are two completely different things. During simulation, just like in real life, your adrenaline is pumping and you can hurt someone.

The point is that you shouldn't try to severely hurt or kill someone who is not actually a threat. If someone is just stopping you on the sidewalk to ask you a question, you don't want to smash their toes or knee them in the groin. If they're just standing in your way and don't seem dangerous, don't blow their shin out or try to stab them in the eyes. If you're not sure whether someone is attempting to hurt you or not, get away from them as quickly as you can. Don't take chances, but don't overreact either. You don't want to end up being the one accused of assault.

If someone stops you when you are riding your bike and you get off your bike to talk to them, you don't need to immediately kick them in the groin. You keep your bike between you and the other person until you know they are harmless. If they ask you the time and then they try to hurt you or abduct you, you can now use your bike as part of your self-defense strategy.

If they start to grab your bike and you realize, *Wait, they don't really need to know what time it is; they want to take my bike*, then you can use the hammer fist move to force them to release their grip on your bike, or your arm, or both.

Use common sense with this. Keep your actions to what is appropriate for the situation. If it's helpful, you can remember the biblical phrase "an eye for an eye and a tooth for a tooth." Anything beyond that might be considered an attack, not self-defense.

If you are in your 10 percent and you are in danger of physical harm, then don't worry about hurting them too much. Use your personal weapons to protect yourself by all means available and escape.

There are other factors to consider when assessing a situation and figuring out the proper response needed. Are you alone in a remote area where no one can hear you? Is there some other way you can escape? Are there cars driving by that you can flag down? If there are people in cars, do whatever is necessary to let people know you're in trouble and need help. Even if you don't see anyone nearby, there may be someone within shouting distance. Somebody could be coming down a trail nearby or about to walk around the corner, so yell, "Stop! Stay back! Get away from me!" as loudly as you can.

And here's another thing: if there's no one around, I would ask you why you're riding your bike where there are no other people and no cell phone service. You should know enough to never do that; that's just not smart.

ESCAPE IS ALWAYS THE BEST MOVE

Everything that we teach and do in personal safety is designed to escape the situation. If you do a hammer fist to their forearm and they momentarily let go, you then have to immediately escape and run to safety. I advise you not to run after them and try to hurt them more. Just leave the situation and do whatever you need to do to take care of yourself, and/or call the police if you feel your life is in danger.

What if you walked out of the gym and saw a suspicious-looking man standing next to his van parked next to your car. The van's side door was slid open, and the man appeared to be getting something from inside the van. Would you keep walking to your car and put yourself in a situation where the minute you get to the driver's side door, they turn around and grab you and throw you into the van? No, you would assess the situation first. Maybe it's a father strapping his baby into their car seat, or he's just putting his gym bag into the van. The van's side door was slid open, and the man appeared to be getting something from inside the van. If something like this happened to you, would you keep walking to your car and put yourself in a situation where the minute you get to the driver's side door, they turn around and grab you and throw you into the van? No, you would assess the situation first. Maybe it's a father strapping his baby into their car seat, or he's just putting groceries into the van. Assess what's going on, then make the decision to proceed to your car or wait. If the van looks dirty and unkempt, with curtains or paper covering the windows, then clearly that is a sign that you should not go to your car. You should wait until the van leaves or ask a security guard to walk you to your vehicle. If there is no one around, I would wait.

Let's say you haven't read this book and you're walking to your car. You're thinking, *I'm going to have to ask him to move out of the way so I can get in my car.* You get there, and before you can ask him anything, he grabs you, and you're struggling to get free now. You have to use all of your options so you can escape: a heel kick to the groin, an elbow strike to the face, fingers/spear strike to the eyeballs, anything to escape and go get help. Most importantly, use your strong voice to get people's attention.

I'll never forget a time on the news many years ago, before cell phones and wireless landlines, when a student at the local university was taking courses in the evenings. She was in her thirties or forties, and one of her professors became very fond of her. He eventually became romantically interested in her even though he was married and had kids. He found out where she lived, snuck into her house, and tried to rape her. He surprised her by jumping on top of her on her bed. As she fought back to get him off her, she managed to reach over to the bedside table and grabbed her old landline rotary phone to call 911. (Cell phones didn't exist in the early nineties.) But then, instead of calling 911, she took it and beat him with it on his face until he was knocked unconscious. In her panicked state, she tried to use the phone to call the police, but she had just broken it, so she ran to her neighbor's house and called the police. On the news, they showed his sorry-ass face, and he looked like he'd been in a boxing match with Mike Tyson. There was no way to know what he was capable of doing, so she would have, more than likely, not been in trouble. The law is nuanced about these issues, but if you trust your gut and rely on your common sense, you'll know to what degree you need to fight back.

OTHER TOOLS FOR SELF-DEFENSE

People often ask me about using pepper spray, and I tell them that if they want to purchase and carry pepper spray, they have to be prepared to know how to use it. The best way to get yourself prepared is to take a course in self-defense that includes the use of pepper spray. If a class is not available and you still want to carry pepper spray, my suggestion is to purchase two canisters: one to practice with and one to keep with you for when you need to use it to defend yourself. When practicing with your extra pepper spray, please do not use your pets or younger siblings as your assailant. Make a target with paper and put it on a tree or fence in your yard.

Remember, if you find yourself in the unfortunate situation of having to defend yourself physically, don't panic. Shift from one technique to another or a combination of techniques until the attacker loosens their grip. If the assailant still doesn't let go, keep resisting until their grip is loosened, then grab a finger(s) and sharply bend backward. Finally, do whatever you can to escape.

Remember, you have options. You can land a "hammer fist" to their forearm to make them let go of your wrist or your purse. You can kick their groin to keep them from running after you. If there are other people nearby, you can yell, "No! Leave me alone! Stay back!" Anyone who hears this will know something's wrong and know you need help. There are options, but the goal is to decide which option you should use and when. This requires awareness of your situation and the opportunities available to you.

The goal is always to escape.

Other than walking home alone at night, Sara did everything right, and in the end, she escaped what could have easily been a mugging or worse, being raped. It's important to notice that just one of these defensive moves isn't always enough. You have to keep trying. Use your common sense and your instincts to find a way to escape.

Our instincts to avoid a situation, or even just to sharpen

our awareness and proceed with caution, are the subject of the next chapter. We will unveil one of the most important tools you have, and like your personal weapons, it's something you carry around 24/7: your gut.

CHAPTER 5: STAY A.W.A.R.E. TAKEAWAYS

- Don't use force or attack someone if you're not being attacked or in close danger of being attacked.
- Escape is always the best answer.
- If you can't escape, use the tools in this chapter to protect yourself and get away.

FEAR IS YOUR FRIEND

Sara and Bri came out of the Target near their campus one sunny afternoon. It was early spring, but it was already quite warm out. They both had a couple of bags filled with dorm room snacks and beverages and were giddily reviewing the events of the night before.

"Mark was so funny last night," Bri laughed. "I think he likes you."

"Nah," Sara said. "He was just drunk." They both laughed. And then Sara stopped laughing and squinted her eyes toward the car. She was checking out the white van parked to the left of her Toyota 4Runner. The side sliding door on the beat-up van was open, and a man was standing there just outside the vehicle, leaning inside as if he was getting something out of it.

Sara stopped walking toward her car.

"Whoa, hold up," she said.

Bri's eyes went wide in amusement. "What? It's just some weirdo."

"Yeah, he's a weirdo," Sara said. "But let's wait a minute and see if he leaves."

Bri stood there impatiently. "C'mon, Sara. What are you paranoid about now? Let's go. I'm melting in this sun, and so are the mochis."

"I don't think so, Bri," Sara said. "We're going to go back inside for a few and wait till he's gone."

"Why? I'm sure it's fine." Bri whined.

Sara turned to her with a sharp look and pursed lips. She meant business.

"Well, I'm not," Sara said.

Bri rolled her eyes and reluctantly followed Sara back to the store. But on the way, she looked over her shoulder and saw the man turn around and look at her. *He is kind of creepy*, she thought.

"Fine, let's go get Starbucks," Bri said with a sigh.

As they stood in line for afternoon Refreshers, Sara explained to Bri that a strange-looking guy with a van right by your driver's side door is a red flag. The guy could be trying to abduct someone by quickly shoving them into the van and taking off. Bri was skeptical; she came from a rich neighborhood where every home was gated and crime was low and never considered these kinds of things. She just shrugged. She couldn't relate to Sara's constant state of being on guard about crime prevention and personal safety, but after her experiences with her grandmother's necklace and the creeps in the garage at Christmas, she didn't feel the need to take any more chances either.

Since Sara had a background in self-defense and was raised to stay A.W.A.R.E., she knew enough to listen to her gut instincts when something felt wrong.

We've talked quite a bit about the need to maintain awareness of our external surroundings. You must look around, keep an eye out, and assess the safety of wherever you are to stay in your Yellow Color Code and avoid becoming a victim. In Chapter 1, we discussed two different types of awareness: external awareness and another, equally important type of awareness—internal awareness. This is the kind of awareness that comes from within, from our gut. Call it intuition, call it instinct, call it "something's not quite right"—our intuition is rarely wrong.

I once had an experience at a drive-through that will give you a perfect example of this. For the last fifteen years, three of my closest friends from college and I have gotten together once a year for a weekend girls trip. One year, we were all meeting up at South Lake Tahoe, and I had driven up there with one of them who lived near me in Castro Valley. It was about 9:00 p.m., and we were just on the outskirts of Sacramento, about to head into the mountains before reaching South Lake Tahoe and our hotel. We stopped at a Kentucky Fried Chicken drive-through because we were hungry and she needed to go to the bathroom. We went through the drive-through, and as I was paying the guy at the drive-through, I asked him if he had a bathroom inside.

"Yes," he said. "But unfortunately we're closed. Only the drive-through is open."

Then he looked in the car and saw that it was only my friend and me inside. I went to pay, and when he took my money, he touched my hand in a flirty, weird, and inappropriate way, which gave me the creeps. "Why don't you just park the car, and we'll let you in? Then you can use the bathroom," he said. I looked in the window of the KFC and saw that the other worker was also a male, and the cashier called out to him to let him know what was happening. "A couple of gals are going to come in and use the restroom," he told his coworker.

Again, it felt a little strange.

Another person might not have taken note of this, but I've seen too much to let anything slip by me. There was something off here.

"Thank you," my friend said to the cashier. And then we started driving up to the next window to get our food. As our car inched forward, I recognized a feeling: something was not quite right, and that was enough for me. I decided we were not going to get our food; we were going to get the heck out of there, and immediately. I floored it and drove right out.

Naturally, my friend was not happy with me. "What are you doing?" she asked.

"We're getting out of here," I said. It didn't matter that she had to pee; I did not have a good feeling about him or that place. I did not even want to eat the food or drink the drink because who knows what they could have put in there. I would have rather pulled over to the side of the road than get stuck in that KFC with whatever might happen. We stopped at a nearby Denny's, and she ran in to go to the bathroom. We drove the rest of the way hungry, but we were safe.

You have to think before you act. Should we go to a closed-down drive-through with only two guys in it? Or should we get to a twenty-four-hour Denny's full of lights and people?

She mentioned it to our other friends several times over the weekend, so everyone knew how "mean" I was, but I didn't care. I kept saying, "Girl, you don't even want to know what they could have done to us if we'd gone in there."

In order to have internal awareness, we need to start with external awareness. If we are oblivious to what's going on around us and we're not even conscious that there could be a problem, we won't get the intuitive hit that can serve as a warning.

External awareness can be learned and developed over

time. You quickly learn not to leave your purse visible in the car. You've also learned along the way what some clear signs of danger are. Internal awareness can be developed through repeatedly listening to your "inner voice." The more you listen to it, the more your gut will send you messages.

TRUST THOSE INSTINCTS

In Gavin de Becker's book *The Gift of Fear*, which we discussed earlier, listening to her intuition saved that woman's life. She'd had a little bit of hesitation, a little bit of that gut feeling, but because the man was so friendly and nice, she ignored her gut and let him carry her groceries up to her apartment. I would advise that you never trust a stranger in that way, no matter how nice they seem.

If she had been in a dark alley and saw him, and he asked her if he could help, she probably wouldn't have trusted him. But she was out in daylight, out in the open, and everything seemed fine. So even if the back of her mind was telling her, *Something's not quite right*, she went ahead and let him help her and ended up getting raped.

After he sexually assaulted her, it was a different story. The man hadn't tied her up, and he left her in the bedroom while he went to the kitchen to get some water. But she had seen him shut the window before he left the room, and her gut shouted, *Get out now or you will be killed*, so she did everything within her power to get out, and she survived.

If your gut tells you something isn't right, don't do it. You may disappoint or unintentionally reject another person by not doing it, but you can make it up to them another time. Like my drive-through experience, you can find somewhere else to go to the bathroom.

When my sister and I left the supermarket on Thanksgiving Eve and had to steer clear of the screaming lunatic, it was my intuition that told me he was not a threat. My sister was in her Black Color Code. She was so frozen with fear and overwhelmed by the situation that she acted inappropriately by running by the man and yelling almost as crazily as the man had been.

Fear helps you stay aware, and awareness helps you feel your fear. They are interdependent. You want to be aware of your fear, so you have to have some level of awareness to be in touch with your fear. This is the 90 percent. You need that awareness, information, and knowledge in order to respond appropriately to certain threats and threat levels. Fear can only be your friend if you know what to do with it. This means using your common sense and making wise choices.

MAKE FRIENDS WITH YOUR FEAR

I like fear. Fear is my friend. If you don't feel fear in your life, then you're probably not doing very much. You're just staying home too much. It's okay to feel fear; it means you're out there as much as others. And if you do it with awareness and a prepared mindset, your tool belt filled with self-defense strategies, you'll be able to handle most anything that comes your way.

You can't let fear run your life. But how do you decide when something is too risky and needs to be avoided or if it is safe for you to proceed? Your external awareness will guide you to the red flags that connect with and lead to intuitive guidance.

In the example of the white van in the parking lot, the fact that the man was standing outside his van looking in through the open sliding side door was a red flag for me. If he's bent over with his head inside and his body outside, my intuition will see that as potentially dangerous. He could be totally innocent and simply looking for his reusable grocery bags. But I will not take that chance. These are the times when you have to make a decision based on your hunch. Is it worth it to doubt your hunches and be trapped in his van a few moments later, drugged from his chloroform and lying there helpless, thinking, *Why did I think he was harmless?*

I'm not going to do that, and you shouldn't either. I will not go to my car while he's there and risk getting thrown into that van through the open side door.

Vehicles in general have the capacity to do a lot of harm. You can be trapped inside one, or you can be forcibly blocked or stopped by one, or your tires can be slashed by a metal object intentionally placed in the road in a bad part of town.

We often think of parking garages as safer and more secure because you are parking inside a structure, but they can actually be more dangerous, sometimes, than parking on a street or out in a lot. As Bri found out, garages have dark areas, and sometimes shady people hang out in them to commit crimes. If there are no other people nearby when you walk into the parking garage alone to get your car, you're making yourself vulnerable to a crime. Especially if it's late at night, consider parking somewhere well lit where you'll be visible to others.

I travel in and out of the Phoenix airport a lot, and in the summer months when the weather is atrociously hot, I opt to park in the parking garage to keep my car out of the hot sun. Sometimes there are people walking to or from the parking garage to the airport tram, but other times it's just me. I am always aware when getting out of my vehicle and taking my luggage out of my trunk. I look to make sure I am not parked next to a car with someone sitting in it, and if so, I move to another parking space. I will then walk in the middle of the aisles and not in between cars. I am not on my phone. I am on high alert because I am in a vulnerable location and still in my Yellow Color Code. As soon as I get closer to where there are people, I'm still not on my phone until I get to a safe location where I can use my phone if I need to.

Hiking trails are another place we don't often think of as risky. Many people love to hike, and sometimes they hike in remote areas where there is no cell service. They love it because it is isolated and peaceful. They love it so much they overlook the danger. Because I teach self-defense, I wonder, *What if something happens? Who will know where I am?* No one. It's too risky to hike alone on a remote trail with no cell service. There are rapists; there are serial killers. You have a very slim chance of encountering one, of course, but remote places are known to be targeted by these kinds of deranged criminals.

One time, when I was working at Cal State University, East Bay, for example, an incident occurred just outside of the perimeter of the campus. A female student was walking to class, and she took a shortcut through the bushes on a dirt path that ran between the campus and this remote area. This was a short trail out of the way that some students used as a shortcut to get to their classes from the parking lot. She was heading for class and was attacked. The assailant punched her out, dragged her into the bushes, and raped her.

Another time, a woman was jogging around the campus, and as she started jogging on a path that led toward the sta-dium track, she was attacked and raped. Isolated places are risky, for women especially.

The point is not to scare you (too much) but to give you my advice: if you're going hiking, take a buddy. Tell people where you're going. If you are set on hiking alone, then purchase *and learn how to use* pepper spray, which burns an attacker's eyes so much that they are temporarily blinded. Learn how to use this defensive tool before you might need to use it. If you don't know how to use it, it could end badly for you because they might turn the spray against you. Pepper spray is legal in all US states; however, different states have different policies about how much you can buy and where you can buy it.

FACING REALITY

Remember the story of my relatives during our family earthquake preparation? A couple of them literally did not want to think about it. And yet an earthquake is coming in our area. It's not about "if" it will happen but "when."

Listening to your gut is not the only internal shift you need to make; it's also important to have the courage and willingness to face the reality that it's dangerous out there and you need to be prepared. Face the reality of a situation and don't go into Black, where you are frozen in fear, or White, where you are oblivious and completely unaware. The thing is, you are so much safer and will be so much better off if you face the fear, face the danger, and assess it so you know how to handle it. Without doing that, you put yourself in so much more danger because you won't be prepared at all when something happens.

Don't overreact out of fear. In fearful situations, our senses sharpen if we are aware enough. Our alertness increases. This heightened focus can be valuable in high-stakes situations. When you feel something is off, your body fills with tension and your mind focuses on the situation. Unfortunately, some people don't respond appropriately in fear-inducing moments. They don't know how to deal with an emergency. They may go into their Black Color Code, thinking catastrophically and not thinking about how to get out of a situation. It's important to know how to correctly assess a dangerous situation and how to respond to it.

Take the Heimlich maneuver, for example. I believe that everyone should know how to do this, but they don't. If someone is choking and you don't know how to help them, you'll go into freeze mode, not knowing what to do.

One time, I was at a steak house with my family. There were about ten of us there, and my sister started choking. I used to be a first aid and CPR instructor for my department. I know that the first thing you need to do when someone is choking is to make sure that they are still able to breathe. If they're coughing, they can breathe. However, some people will just panic if something is stuck in their airway. In this situation, the only way you can tell they're not breathing is if they can't talk at all and are in extreme panic. If they can't talk and no breath can come out of their mouth, what do you do? The Heimlich maneuver. I didn't know if anyone at our table knew the Heimlich maneuver. I knew it, but I also knew that since my sister was trying to cough the obstruction out, she could breathe. "Just let her get it out; let her cough it up," I said.

Some family members were rushing out of their chairs to help her. I had to say, "Hold on. She's okay."

"She doesn't look okay," a family member anxiously replied.

"She is okay," I said. "She's not choking. She has something stuck in her throat, and she is panicking. Let her cough it out."

If you don't know how to assess the situation, then you're not in a good position to solve the problem. My family members had great intentions, but they might have made things worse if they'd given her the Heimlich when she didn't need it. I'm not trying to brag or take credit for anything; I'm just trying to make the point that you need to know what to do in these kinds of emergencies.

In this situation, I was using both my external awareness and my internal awareness. My gut told me that it might not be necessary to give her the Heimlich right away, so I watched and used my knowledge about choking protocol and my assessment of the situation to determine that we should not do the Heimlich on her.

It comes back to the Assess in A.W.A.R.E. Accurate, appropriate assessment of an emergency takes knowledge and information. Let's say you want to apply this to your life as a young adult just out of the nest. What if someone is showing signs of alcohol overdose? If you're newly out of the nest, you won't necessarily know how to deal with that. You might go into your Black Color Code, your freeze mode. But instead, you'd be better off staying focused and assessing the situation, even if it's a stressful moment. Figure out what needs to be done and call for help. In the example of an apparent alcohol overdose, you might want to call an ambulance, just in case.

In fearful situations, our senses sharpen and our awareness increases. This heightened focus can be valuable in high-stakes environments. The fear we feel in these situations is not just from thinking about what we're seeing and trying to figure out what we should do. The fear is also physical. We will automatically tense up, feel the hair on the back of our neck tingle, and experience an immediate adrenaline rush designed to help us with fight or flight.

DON'T DISMISS YOUR FEAR; LISTEN TO IT

"Fear is your friend" means don't be dumb. Don't be all-trusting of everyone and everything that's going on. Don't dismiss your fear; listen to it. The smallest oversight or impulsive decision, like walking down a dark alley after a couple of drinks at night, can lead to some terrible consequences. You don't have to be paranoid; just be A.W.A.R.E.

When Sara saw the man in the white van next to her car, her mother's voice and her own instincts and knowledge of self-defense made her stop and turn around. She could have made a grave mistake by walking into the situation and ultimately getting kidnapped, assaulted, or worse.

For college students and working young adults, your personal safety will often come down to staying aware wherever you are and listening to your gut. This applies to your time spent in the dorms and the relative safety of the campus itself, as well as when you are out and about in your city or town. In the next chapter, we will look at some more common safety risks you may encounter when you're out in the wild of the real world.

CHAPTER 6: STAY A.W.A.R.E. TAKEAWAYS

- Face your fears by listening to them so you don't become a victim.
- Don't overreact out of fear—sometimes that can make things worse.
- Trust your instincts!

BE A GOOD WITNESS

It's not just young women who are victims of assault; it can happen to men as well.

Jack was a seventeen-year-old freshman at a large urban university. He was an intelligent kid, but he grew up in a small town in the mountains of Colorado, and he was short on street smarts. He moved into the dorm with a student he met through the university's online roommate finder, and they got along well.

Landing at a large university in the city was a major change for Jack, and he immediately fell into the college party scene. Braxton and Jack were both athletic, and they went to the gym together every day after classes. They also both liked going out and partying, and soon they were part of a larger group of guys who were hitting the gym and the parties several times a week, and because many of them, including Jack, had fake IDs, they were also getting into bars.

One night, Jack and Braxton and some of the other guys were out at a bar, drinking Long Island iced teas and getting hammered. Jack and one of the other guys stayed later than the rest, and then Jack started feeling the effects of too much alcohol and decided he was going to walk back to the dorm. He had gotten half a block away when he encountered a man and a woman, not college students, but locals from the neighborhood, in a loud, angry shouting match. The man, who looked like he could be a bodybuilder, was pushing the woman and not allowing her to get into her car. She was yelling at him to leave her alone.

Jack froze. He had no idea how to respond, but he felt he should do something, anything, to help the woman. He approached the couple but kept his distance and said, "Hey! Leave her alone. Let her go. Can't you see she wants you to leave her alone?" The burly guy stopped what he was doing and let go of the woman long enough for her to get into her car and drive off. He turned to Jack and nodded his head as if to say, *Okay, it's over*, and then walked off in another direction, away from Jack. Jack watched him go, but the man went about half a block and then turned around and ran toward Jack. This man was big. He tackled Jack to the ground and started ruthlessly punching him in the face and gut, saying things like "You want to get in my business?" and "Think you're a big man, huh?"

Jack's remaining friend came out of the bar and saw what was going on. He ran back in and brought some other kids from inside the bar to come help, and they all pulled the man off of Jack. The man took off, and a battered Jack accepted his friends' help to get him back to the dorm. In the morning, he woke up with a dislocated jaw that he thought might be broken, a cut above his eye, and several bruised ribs. It would be many days before he could get back to his classes.

Unfortunately, Jack had not participated in the self-defense seminar the university had sponsored for students at the beginning of the semester. If he had, he would have learned all about how to be a good witness, and he would never have tried to be a hero and gotten himself involved in that confrontation.

DON'T BE A HERO

I realize it is difficult, especially for a healthy young man with pride, to watch a woman be harassed or assaulted and not want to intervene. But the best way to assist in this situation is not to get nearer to the altercation. It is to get your phone out and call for help.

There is strength in numbers, especially if there is a crime in progress. You can still be a hero: call 911, get a description, and gather other people to help you. Don't go in alone.

If you want to assist the police department and help the community reduce the amount of crime, the best way to do it is not to try and apprehend the perpetrator if you are not trained in doing so. That could be detrimental to you and others around you. You may end up sacrificing your life and possibly other people's lives as well. Don't be a hero; just be a credible witness. Be someone who helps law enforcement find the perpetrator and prevent them from committing any more crimes. Being a good witness means staying safe so that you can provide the authorities with as much information as you can gather.

How do we become good witnesses? There are many, many ways, and we will unpack them in this chapter. But two of the most crucial and immediate ways are to call the authorities and to get a good description. These should always be your first actions.

Calling the authorities is as easy as 911. If there is a crime in progress or a life-threatening situation, always call 911. If it is not one of these two things, the 911 operator will reroute you to the appropriate department so the proper authorities can be dispatched to the scene.

DESCRIBING THE SUSPECT

Getting a good description of the suspect involves several details and is complex, especially when you are frazzled from what you just witnessed. Gathering your thoughts and focusing on a witness description can be challenging, but here are some things to focus on.

Are there any special facial or hair features, such as scars; eye color; a distinctive nose, mouth, or chin; a ponytail; or a crew cut?

Is their skin color light or dark? It might be hard to tell, but do your best to note their skin color, height, weight, and hair color.

Maybe they use slang or have an accent. Do they sound like they're from the South? Or the East Coast? Europe? Take a picture on your phone of their clothing if you can. If not, then just make a note of it. What color is it? Loose or tight-fitting? What type of clothing are they wearing? What about their shoes? What color and style are they? Getting a description of their shoes is one of the most important details because if the suspect is being chased by the police, they will most likely dump their jacket or hat or beanie, but they'd be stupid to dump their shoes.

Did you see if they have any personal items on them, like a backpack, knife, or gun?

If they are holding something, is it with their left hand or right hand?

If you see them walking or running away, do they have a distinct walk, such as a limp, or are they bowlegged? Where was "the direction of flight"—meaning which way did they go?

The more you gather a mental picture of all of these details, the more you will aid law enforcement in their investigation and help them capture the perpetrator.

THE VEHICLE

Next, get a description of the vehicle, if there is one. This is key! If they flee in a vehicle, note the color and style of the car, how many people are in it, and their direction of flight (meaning which way did it go?). Was it older or newer? Sedan or SUV? Of course, if you can get the license plate or even some of the numbers or letters of the license plate, that is the golden ticket. Sometimes criminals will swap out their license plate for someone else's; however, some criminals are dumb and don't do that. Just know that it is not always reliable information.

THE BE A GOOD WITNESS EXERCISE

In my presentations to high school and college students, I teach young people to be a good witness in case they ever need to be questioned about an investigation.

First, I put three photos of three different suspects up on the screen, one at a time. They are all suspects in a crime that was just committed. One is female, and two are males. The first photo I show for five to seven seconds, then I ask the students to describe the suspect from head to toe and if they notice anything important other than height, weight, ethnicity, and direction of flight. Often, nobody even notices that he's carrying a gun in his left hand, indicating that not only is he armed, but he is also left-handed. Use the bank's counter height to estimate the height of the suspect. I have the students look at the counter in front of the bank tellers and decide how tall the bank robbers are. I ask what their skin color is. Because they often have masks on, and sometimes hoodies or hats, it's a little difficult to tell sometimes.

I also have three different photos of three different vehicles. I throw one up on the screen for five seconds and then take it down. Then I ask the students to describe it—the color, the type of car, how many doors it has, and what direction it was heading.

The purpose is to help the students learn how to identify and describe an assailant (and possibly their vehicle) without getting into a confrontation with them so that if they see a crime unfolding, they can be a good, credible witness. You can try this while in line at the grocery store—if you see someone who looks slightly suspicious, you can try and retain these descriptive details in your memory. Doing this will help you to be a good witness in the event of a crime and help you to practice in case you encounter one in the future.

There is so much that law enforcement can use from a description of a suspect and a vehicle. It's the small details that can make a huge difference in the search for the suspect and vehicle. For instance, if you see someone taking a laptop in the library, you're going to take careful note of their clothing, height, race, sex, and any other distinguishing characteristics. You can make a mental note of everything about their appearance and behavior you see. Because you're reading this book, you're not going to jump in and be a hero by intervening.

I also share some tricks with my students to help them

describe and identify people. If you're in a 7-Eleven or similar mini-mart, know that convenience stores are robbed more often than most businesses. To help catch the suspects, these stores have height strips on the doorframe with basic height measurements between five feet and seven feet so that as the suspect runs out, a witness can determine that they are about six foot two, or whatever it is, and report their approximate height.

Once you get the description of the person, note which way they walked. Did they cross the street? Did they get into a car? If you didn't see the suspect get into a car, did you see a car outside?

Let's say an assailant shot the clerk in one of these stores. If you witness this, you might remember that you saw a red car parked in front of the store right before it happened. This information could be extremely helpful in the investigation.

Many cities these days have cameras on almost every major street corner. If police know the direction the car went, the real-time crime center, which watches these cameras, will look through the footage at those intersections and be able to tell the detectives which red cars went through that intersection within that thirty-minute window. In 2023, I attended the California Crime Prevention Officers' Association (CCPOA) conference, and a speaker discussed these real-time crime centers (RTCC) and told us how they work in her police agency. Not all agencies have an RTCC, but those that do use technologies and data analysis to give officers immediate intelligence during ongoing incidents and investigations. They use data from sources like CCTV, license plate readers, and computer-aided dispatch to enable faster responses.

For civilians, beyond describing the suspect and the direction of flight of the vehicle, it's difficult to be a good witness.

But there are many small nuances you can try to catch, such as a suspect's speech, the way they walk, their height, and so on. Try to notice as much as you can. The more information you gather, the more tools law enforcement will have to work with to solve the crime. This is being a good witness and a true hero because you are truly helping law enforcement in the best and safest way.

YOUR TURN

Now I'm going to ask you to try the same exercise I give in my courses. You will be doing a good witness memory test, and I'm going to give you three scenarios.

Before you click on the QR code for your exercise, I will give you the scenario. Describe what you saw in the video and try to remember as many details as you can. Sometimes you'll be seeing a person; other times it's a vehicle. If it's a person, try to remember height, weight, sex, race, hat or clothing, if they had a gun, and direction of flight. If it's a vehicle, describe the color, make, model and as much detail as possible, and the direction of flight. Let's do this!

SCENARIO 1

You are at a gas station convenience store getting a fountain drink. Your back is turned away from the rest of the store. You hear a commotion, and you turn around to look. You see a person running out of the store and getting into a car.

Suspect Description

1. Hair color
2. Eye color

3. Skin color
4. Clothing (also shoes)
5. Height and weight
6. Scars or other facial marks
7. Voice/accent/lisp
8. Possessions

Vehicle Description

1. Color
2. Make and model (e.g., Ford Bronco)
3. Number of passengers
4. Direction of flight

SCENARIO 2

You are in your vehicle, parking at a grocery store, and before you get out of your vehicle, you witness someone robbing a woman of her purse as she is putting groceries in the trunk of her car. She is playing tug-of-war with her purse, and finally she lets it go, and the assailant runs off between cars toward Main Street.

Suspect Description

1. Hair color
2. Eye color
3. Skin color
4. Clothing (also shoes)
5. Height and weight
6. Scars or other facial marks
7. Voice/accent/lisp
8. Possessions
9. Direction of flight

SCENARIO 3

You are at a gas station pumping gas, and you hear gunshots nearby. Seconds later, a car drives past the gas station at a high rate of speed. Before you can finish pumping gas, you hear police sirens and the gas station is filled with cop cars.

Vehicle Description

1. Color
2. Noticeable characteristics of the vehicle (ski rack, bumper stickers, tinted windows, vehicle damage)
3. Make and model (e.g., Ford Bronco)
4. Number of passengers (if possible)
5. License plate
6. Direction of flight

Click this QR code to get started!

THE RISKS OF JUMPING IN

Being a good witness not only helps law enforcement catch the suspect; it can help you too. Instead of jumping in and trying to intervene, you can stay safe and just collect some data in your mind or Notes app. This is crucial because serious risks are involved in trying to be a hero instead of being a good witness.

Several years ago, I hosted a community academy class, where my department offered a series of classes for the community to attend so they could learn about our city and the duties of each department. This academy for the community helped them understand the functions of each department. One of our speakers was an owner of the security company down the street, and at the end of the academy, all the attendees got to go into their shooting range simulation. It was one of the highlights of the academy because the attendees got to see what it's like for an officer to be in a situation where they have to use their weapon on someone. The owner of the security company had asked me why my partner and I, who are nonsworn crime prevention specialists, don't carry concealed weapons, since there are times where we have to be out in the community and, at times, we run into unruly people. He also stated that the county sheriff would definitely approve our request to carry (which is a CCW). At first I thought it would be a cool idea.

Days later I was talking to my coworker, who is a sworn officer, and I started telling him my thoughts on the possibility of applying for a CCW. Then I told him I was worried that if I did get one, I would feel like I had to save everyone! He said his rule is to only use your weapon if you or your family is in imminent danger and it's a matter of life or death. I still wasn't comfortable with that because I am not trained in that capacity. I wouldn't know what to do in a situation that involves either saving lives or taking someone's life. It could turn against me, and then I would be liable as a result of my actions.

My coworker told me, "You don't have to be a hero; just be a good witness. You have the skills, just like all of us, to stay out of danger, just not the skills to apprehend a suspect. Just be a good witness." So I opted not to apply for a CCW and focused on 90 percent of my safety.

When the man Jack encountered on the street started walking away, Jack felt good. He thought all was well and felt like he had been a hero. But in a few short seconds, everything changed, and as it turned out, he could have been killed. Fortunately he wasn't, but he was debilitated for weeks. This happens to be a common situation for young people who have left the nest and are out in the wild of the real world. A guy and a girl are fighting about something, another guy comes in and gets involved, and bad things can happen. If you think about it, since the guy is already attacking a girl, there is something seriously wrong with him. So it's best to keep clear. Call 911 and let the attacker know that the cops are on their way. This could stop him from continuing his attack without anyone else getting hurt.

Just be a good witness. As we've seen, even law enforcement officers choose to stay out of an altercation and instead use the time to record the details about the people involved—in their minds or in writing. Law enforcement officers are well-trained to do this, and they have a remarkable ability to capture the descriptive details about people and their activities. We can learn from them in many ways; they have a treasure trove of knowledge about how to protect themselves. In the next chapter, I'll share some of the many ways cops take action to keep themselves safe in their line of work and how you can use the same knowledge to stay A.W.A.R.E.

> **CHAPTER 7: STAY A.W.A.R.E. TAKEAWAYS**
>
> - Don't be a hero; be a good witness.
> - Get as many details and descriptions of the assailant as you can.
> - Being a good witness can save lives and solve crimes; trying to be a hero can get you hurt.

CHAPTER 8

THINK LIKE A LEO

When Bri and Sara found out that their favorite up-and-coming band was coming to town, they decided to get tickets. The show was going to be at the largest venue in the city, and it was sold out. When concert day finally arrived, Sara insisted they get there early so they could park close to the stadium and not have to walk a long way after the show. Once inside, Sara was overwhelmed by the size of the stadium.

"Wow, look at all the people here! This place is humongous," she mumbled as they made their way inside and found their seats. They went and bought some drinks and snacks while they waited for the show to start. From the moment they arrived at the stadium, a safety announcement would come on about every fifteen to twenty minutes on several of the giant screens, showing people in their respective sections where to exit if an evacuation was needed. It clearly showed a map of the stadium, indicating all the exit routes from each section. Sara finally looked up at the screen and started calculating which exit route would be best, but then she noticed Bri was on her phone, not paying any attention at all.

"Hey, let's watch this in case something happens and we need to escape. We need to know what our escape route is." Bri rolled her eyes. Sometimes Sara's safety stuff was a little too much, she was thinking.

"Um, why?" Bri asked with a slightly snotty tone.

"Because I want you to," Sara said flatly. "Or else I'll have to leave you behind if something happens," she added. "Come on, let's watch it together so we both know. Just in case."

Bri looked at the TV screen. "Ohhh-kaaay," she said.

"So we're in the fourth row of this section, so all we'd have to do is get to the first row and then head to the right."

"Nothing's going to happen," Bri insisted.

"Probably not," Sara said. "But we have to be prepared anyway, just in case the shit hits the fan and we have to get the hell out of Dodge! Are you with me?"

Along with having ER doctors as parents, Sara was also a cop show fanatic who watched all the best police procedurals on YouTube or TV every chance she got. This is another reason why she had such a law enforcement officer (LEO) mentality. She had learned to think like a LEO. She knew if there were any police officers there, they would be doing the same thing—figuring out how to protect themselves in case of an emergency.

Sara looked up to the top of the stadium. Could there be any active shooters up there somewhere? She couldn't really tell. But if there were, she planned, she and Bri would duck under their seats. She felt the base of the seat and decided it was pretty sturdy. It could probably stop a bullet. Satisfied that she was fully prepared, she sat back and enjoyed the show.

The cop mentality is a complex web of precautions and

procedures police officers have in place for almost any situation that could be dangerous. In its simplest form, you can think of it as a safety mentality. If there's a threat of any kind, law enforcement officers are crystal clear on how to respond in a way to help them stay safe. This mindset of having a plan to keep yourself from becoming a victim can easily be adopted and applied by people who have recently moved out of their homes and are now living on their own.

The experiences cops have out in the field and in training give them a wealth of tactics to keep themselves safe, and there's no reason we can't use the same tactics to stay safe ourselves. In this chapter, I'll share a handful of tips that will get you thinking like a law enforcement officer, or LEO, as we call them. In the event that you find yourself on the brink of a risk, or if you ever just want to take extra precautions, you'll now be armed with the A.W.A.R.E. method, which will help you in specific, concrete situations.

Recently, I stopped at a coffee shop. The parking lot had several police cars in it, parked and without anyone in them, so I figured there was a group of police officers having breakfast. I went in and ordered my cappuccino and then, since I recognized a couple of them, walked to the back of the coffee shop to say hello. I noticed right away that they had chosen a table at the far back corner of the room, facing the door. Some of the cops had their backs to me as I approached, so they couldn't see me coming, but immediately, the officers sitting across from them saw me and waved. What most people don't realize is that law enforcement officers have a code for just about everything. When they're sitting in a public place, they always make sure that someone "has their back" if their back is not up against the wall. If an officer isn't sure that someone is watching their back, they might even ask, "You got my back?" This concept is like an old analog clock. If you think of the cops' positioning as the numbers in a circle on a clock and you think of the guys against the wall as the twelve at the top of the clock, then the guys whose backs were toward me would be at the six. Thus, "You got my six?" really means "You got my back?"

Why do officers have a code for everything? It's their language at work, and it's a safety measure among them. Well, that in and of itself is a safety measure among them. There are times when they want to keep the strategy and information hidden from civilians so no one can use that information against them. For example, while at a community event, I was approached by a woman who I felt was very angry with me and the police. After agreeing to speak with her, I verbally signaled one of the officers using a police code. I felt safer speaking with her knowing he was watching me and had my back.

These are all what cops just consider best practices to protect their own safety and each other's. When they are sitting in a restaurant, some of them will always have their back to the farthest wall so they have a clear view of the whole place and the door.

Especially when law enforcement officers are in a large group, they will be sure not to get too involved in their conversation that they are not staying fully aware of their surroundings. As a college student or working young adult, you'll most likely have occasions where you're together with others in a group. Try borrowing this tactic from the police. This is called group awareness, and it's about keeping your awareness broad, inside and outside the group, observing the entire surroundings. They will also use other numbers on a clock to indicate direction, such as three, meaning directly to the right of someone.

SITUATIONAL AWARENESS

It is common knowledge that cops are pros at practicing situational awareness. Situational awareness is simply the ability to notice what's happening around you, understand what it means, and use that information to stay safe and make smart decisions.

It's about staying A.W.A.R.E.—Alert, Watching, Assessing, Responding, and Escaping if necessary. It's not about being paranoid; in fact, that can work against you.

Situational awareness means that you:

- Stay clear of danger
- Keep an eye out for potential problems
- Respond with speed and common sense in an emergency
- Take steps to keep yourself and others safe

EXAMPLES WHEN YOU'RE OUT AND ABOUT

- Noticing someone following you as you walk and crossing the street to confirm
- Paying attention to exits when entering a building
- Seeing a drink left unattended and choosing not to drink from it

EXAMPLES AT HOME

- Realizing a window that was closed is now open
- Noticing a car you don't recognize repeatedly passing your street
- Checking who's at the door before opening it

EXAMPLES WHILE DRIVING

- Watching the behavior of cars around you, not just the one in front
- Seeing brake lights several cars ahead and slowing early
- Recognizing a car that has been behind you through multiple turns

EXAMPLES IN SOCIAL OR PUBLIC SETTINGS

- Spotting someone acting nervous or scanning the room aggressively
- Picking up on a shift in someone's tone before an argument starts
- Noticing someone trying to distract you while another moves closer to your belongings

EXAMPLES ONLINE

- Recognizing a suspicious email asking for urgent personal info
- Checking a link before clicking it
- Noticing when someone adds you online but you don't know them

911 ISN'T ALWAYS THE RIGHT CALL

If you need to call law enforcement, you should know that there are rules about when to call 911 and when you should call the nonemergency number instead. Usually, people think they should just call 911 no matter what the crime is, but sometimes your call won't necessarily be a life-threatening situation or a crime in progress, and in that case, you need to dial the police station for help. Some police agencies are so busy and understaffed that they won't come to your house unless you have information on a suspect. Others will always respond if it is a burglary but not always in other cases.

Sometimes you will need to go to the station and file a report. You should always have your local police department's number on your phone, just in case.

Over the years, 911 has evolved. It used to be that most police agencies only had a handful of call lines. If a widespread emergency broke out and everybody was calling 911, callers would get a busy signal because all of the 911 lines were in use.

In the last few years, a new system has been in development, called Next Generation 911 (NG911), which allows for more calls to be answered and handled more effectively. The system is going to be much more advanced, and even though it isn't fully in place yet, there is a nationwide effort to refine it and get it up and running. The technology will be complex and advanced enough to route calls and share data on a much larger and faster scale in an emergency.

In places where NG911 is not in place yet, if there's a major incident that has occurred, let's say an earthquake or a shooting, everyone and their mother is going to get on the phone and call 911, so unfortunately, a lot of people won't be able to get through.

It's worth mentioning here, too, that there's a defined difference between an emergency and a nonemergency. Remember that a 911 call is for only two things: a life-threatening situation like a fire, serious accident, or medical emergency or a crime in progress. If you wake up and your car has been broken into, don't call 911. Leave those lines open for folks who are in clear and present danger, that is, their life is in danger, or they are witnessing or a victim of an active crime.

DO YOUR RESEARCH

Since you are college aged, most likely you have a computer. You can go online for nonemergencies and file a report. Some agencies may not send an officer to you for a nonemergency call unless you have information on a suspect. Maybe you have taken a picture of a suspect or have video footage from your home cameras. Then they will come to you and make the report as they gather any information you may have about the crime.

Crime prevention is always the primary goal. People often want to know the crime statistics of a particular neighborhood, and that's great. You can go to crime stats sites if you search online. My former agency uses crimemapping.com. Here's the bad news: unfortunately, on college campuses, date rape is often a very common crime. There's also backpack and laptop theft, as well as stalking, reported on most campuses.

Police officers all too often are witnesses to the worst aspects of people's behavior and the consequences of crime. They have a more nuanced understanding of the law, with all of its complexities. They are also problem solvers. If a person is stranded by the side of the road, they are going to think through how to get that person to safety, for instance.

We already discussed the protocol of calling for backup before going into a situation. They also check on each other often during a situation. As we discussed, you now know that it's not smart to leave valuables in your car. Nor should you cover them with an expensive jacket or other accessory that looks nice. Keep a towel in the car, or better yet, take the valuable item with you or put it in the trunk. I have a windshield sunshade in my car and I always use it to cover up anything in the front or back seat. These things are second nature to law enforcement, but they aren't normally considered by civilians. Everything is second nature to LEOs; it's how they live.

THE IMPORTANCE OF HEIGHTENED AWARENESS

One of my police officer colleagues told me a story: his friend, who is also a police officer, was on a flight, and there was an extremely intoxicated man on board. While in the air, the drunk guy got up and tried to open the plane door. His friend and other passengers stopped him and literally sat on him before they restrained him in a seat, strapped by a lot of seat belts. Since that incident, before he gets on a flight, my friend sizes people up during the boarding process so he can see who he could count on if a situation arose. Nothing has ever happened, but he's always aware. This type of heightened awareness is baked into these people's mindsets. These habits are embedded in their day-to-day and minute-to-minute and even second-to-second actions.

My son is a former marine, and even though he's never been a police officer, he is also always aware of his surroundings. He is prepared for the enemy at all times. He has the mindset, too, of knowing where to sit, what to look out for, and how to respond to a threat or potential danger.

In law enforcement or any form of security work, a method called BTA, or behavioral threat assessment, is used to measure the danger level of a situation based on an individual's behavior. The BTA system analyzes the risk factors and helps authorities in charge create a coordinated plan to prevent the crime from happening.

Law enforcement officers are always *assessing*, even if they are off duty and eating dinner with their family at a restaurant or at a concert with a friend. They *watch* for any signs of possible risk. They stay in an alert yet relaxed state when their surroundings appear and feel clear. Of course, they are the main people who will recognize the possibility that a crime could happen, and they are going to *escape* if necessary, but if not, they will assist nearby civilians in escaping while they try to apprehend the suspect or suspects and, if necessary, take them into custody.

It's not just police officers or public safety officers (as they've often been called in recent years) who have a crime prevention and personal safety mindset. LEO is a broad label; law enforcement officers include federal agents, sheriff's deputies, state troopers, and others with the duty to protect and serve. The crime prevention mentality is really the whole point of this book.

Several crime prevention tactics that LEOs use to prevent themselves from becoming victims are also excellent tools for young people leaving the nest. We've looked at situational awareness; in fact, that is the one takeaway I most want you to have from this book. Trust me, outside of a private, safe environment, an officer of the law is not going to be glued to their phone and wearing AirPods, unable to see or hear anything going on around them. They are basically paying attention, noticing who's around, and staying tuned to their intuition or any feelings that something is not quite right.

BE INTENTIONAL ABOUT SAFETY

LEOs also assume a position of authority. Their stance, the confident way they walk, their voice, and even the way they make eye contact all send a message to people around them that says, "Don't even think about it."

They also take many other precautions you can use to keep yourself safe. They don't park in dark or secluded areas, and they always take note of their escape routes.

LEOs take escape very seriously. When I asked one of my police officer friends what he would do if he was off duty and out with his family and observed a fight that involved a gun, he said he might draw his own gun and switch into on-duty mode, but first, he would immediately tell his family to leave. He said his family knows that if he tells them to leave, they leave, no questions asked. They just leave. If an off-duty LEO witnesses people who are just fighting or arguing, they will usually just assess the situation, and when it looks like it has defused, they can become a good witness if needed.

One of the most valuable lessons you can learn from law enforcement is the concept of backup. This is why, early in this book, I strongly encouraged you to always use the buddy system. Never go in alone. Cops are not going to run into a high-risk situation alone; they will wait for backup. For college-aged people, you can also use phone tracking or location sharing, and always let someone know where you're going, especially if you're headed for any place isolated or risky.

The idea of putting your bike in front of you in case a person on the street tries to assault you is also borrowed from law enforcement. They do what they have to do to protect themselves, and sometimes they'll do it proactively, as a "just in case" measure. And I'm sure you've seen plenty of tables or chairs thrown into the faces of criminals in action movies, as the good guys knock out the bad guys.

Law enforcement officers always know when it's time to *escape* as well. If they're outnumbered, they will retreat, get to a safe area, call for backup, and wait until it arrives.

Similarly, you should leave a party and quickly walk away if a fight breaks out, and stay clear of any potentially dangerous people or public disturbances you notice when out on the streets.

IT'S INSTINCTUAL

The police officers I have worked with over the years often spoke of the hair raising on the back of their neck. It's instinctual. I used to lead neighborhood watch meetings, and the cops who were in the room would tell the attendees to always go with their instincts. If the hair on the back of your neck starts to rise, there could be a threat, so stay A.W.A.R.E. A good cop will always be scanning their environment anyway, avoiding tunnel vision, but if their gut is telling them there's a threat nearby, they will not just scan; they will investigate.

You'll often see a LEO use tactical positioning as well. They will stand off-center, at an angle from a suspect or even just a citizen pulled over in a traffic stop. They will avoid getting cornered and keep a safe distance from people they don't know. They make sure they always have a clear line of sight to the nearest exit, and they won't turn their backs to others very much at all.

In the world we live in today, privacy and security have become vital for personal safety. Be discreet. Don't share too much personal information with people you don't know well; these people don't need to know exactly where you live or what your daily routine is. Keep your social media accounts private; there's a reason you have that option. You never know who might be gathering that information to use against you in some way or pose a threat to you.

After decades of working in crime prevention, personal safety, and self-defense, I've developed many instincts that most people don't have. I don't take chances, to put it mildly. For instance, when I was in graduate school at St. Mary's College, I would drive twenty minutes longer than needed to get to school because the faster route included a stretch of two-lane road with hardly any traffic—with sharp curves, wildlife such as deer and boars, and zero cell phone reception in case of emergency. If I hit a wild boar and end up in the ditch, how am I going to get assistance? How do I protect myself? If I chose the two-lane canyon road, I could be caught alone in an emergency with no chance of communication with the outside world. That is why I opted to take the main highway, where there are cars and cell service if I am in need of road-side assistance. Most people would probably not worry about something like that, but after so much time spent seeing all the terrible things that can happen, I do.

Using the street smarts of LEOs and others working in crime prevention is an excellent way to become an expert at ensuring your own personal safety. And in fact, any kind of self-defense or personal safety classes you can take, online or in person, will help you sharpen your awareness and your ability to take more preventive measures.

Ensuring you're not exposing yourself to unnecessary risk doesn't require a badge or a career in self-defense. It's often just a matter of making smart, A.W.A.R.E. decisions. Unsafe incidents are known to occur at concerts, but there are end-less other places I can think of where you should be looking around and identifying your avenues for escape. There's no harm in knowing your exit routes no matter where you are.

The safety habits of a law enforcement officer mostly come down to common sense. There's no price tag on common sense; anyone can use it, and in my opinion, more people should. I like to joke that common sense isn't as common as it used to be, but it's sometimes nothing to joke about. One thing is certain: there's no better time to use it than when you've left the nest and gone into the wild. In the next chapter, we'll explore some of the most common downfalls of leaving home to live on your own, from minor mishaps to the actions that could lead to or prevent you from becoming a victim of a serious crime.

MORE LEAVING THE NEST PLAYBOOK IDEAS

Sara had been raised in a strict home, and because of that, she had strong family values and a lot of knowledge and experience in personal safety. She had also learned self-defense growing up, attending weekly jujitsu classes all through middle school and part of high school. Sara's parents had done a great job of raising her to be wise and stay safe outside the home, and because they had a system in place to take away her and her sister's phones every night at 8:30, Sarah knew how to make wise choices about when to use her phone and when to put it away.

Bri, who was raised with a great deal of freedom and whose parents didn't give her much guidance at all growing up, never had the chance to learn how to make wise choices about how much to look at her phone or when to put it away. While this wasn't dangerous when she was hanging out in her dorm, it had its risks when she was out and about, walking in city streets, sitting on a train, or in public places. This is how, the night that Sara and Bri were coming home on the subway after a night out downtown, where they'd met friends at a bar, someone managed to lift Bri's wallet from her purse. She had been too busy looking at her phone to notice the guy sitting next to her on the train who reached into her purse and quickly lifted it before he got off. When Bri stood up and put her phone in her purse, she realized her wallet was gone. "Oh my God!" she shrieked. She could not believe that she had just lost all her cash and credit cards, her driver's license, and her student ID. All she had left was her phone.

MAKE GOOD CHOICES

It's not just kids who grew up without a lot of rules who need to heighten their awareness of their surroundings by putting down the phone; it's everyone. But college students, immersed in a whole new social life and navigating all-new territory both physically and mentally, are especially vulnerable to overusing their phones to the point of becoming clueless as to what is happening around them.

Sometimes even kids who grew up with very strict rules in their house can go a little too far in the other direction when they move out and live on their own. They have no idea what it's like to have all that freedom. Perhaps they were never even given a phone, so they never learned to manage their usage. If they are never given the chance to regulate themselves at all growing up, they may want to go overboard once they are living away from home. For these kids, it can be tempting to take all their newfound freedom too far.

Think about anything you were restricted from when you

were still living at home, and ask yourself how you are going to make wise choices about that thing in the face of temptation once you're out of the nest and into the wild. Our phones are a great example—they can sometimes consume us so much that they put us in our White Color Code, completely oblivious to any danger or risks to our personal safety.

Remember, just because you're on campus, it doesn't always mean you are safe. Things happen in dorms, parking lots, outside areas all over campus, deserted hallways, and even the gym and the library.

Either on or off campus, inside your apartment (if you aren't on a campus) or outside of it, you can think of the places you go as safety zones and nonsafety zones. Once you step out of your safety zone, say your dorm room or a classroom or the library, into a nonsafety zone, such as the dark, isolated parking structures on the outskirts of campus, you need to be much more aware of your surroundings and take note of any potential risks to your safety. You can even identify your safety zones and make a conscious effort to stay in places where the risks are low as much as possible.

THINK ABOUT YOUR SAFETY NO MATTER WHERE YOU ARE

If you're going to step out into a nonsafety zone, plan ahead and take preventive measures. Knowing there could be potential danger, think it through and be prepared. Always try to bring a buddy when you can.

Remember, 90 percent of your safety is being A.W.A.R.E. Stay Alert, Watch what is happening around you, Assess the things you see or hear nearby, Respond to the danger, and be prepared to Escape if necessary.

Driving; riding public transportation such as a bus, subway, or train; and flying all carry their own unique dangers. These crowded places, filled with strangers from all walks of life, are some of the most crime-filled environments you will find. Public transportation comes with security and personal safety risks that are amplified by the multitude of opportunities for theft and other crimes.

Once you step out of the safety of your family home, like many people, you may end up with your awareness in White, oblivious to any potential danger that might be near. You're in a totally new environment, and when you go to a new place, you never know quite what to expect. You may have no idea that if you cross a particular street into a different neighborhood, it will be dangerous. You may not realize that people get roofied, or that not all rideshare drivers are safe, or that people might actually steal from you, lie to you, or try to trick you. You might not be aware that, sadly, women are raped more frequently than most people think they are.

Things can happen in and around your home, sure, but for the most part, it's a safer place to be. You're living with experienced adults who know how to navigate the dangers of the world to a certain extent. There are so many things you have never thought about before that you need to think about now. It's a major transition, but the great news is you're reading this book. The information in these pages is meant to help you make that transition into an A.W.A.R.E. young adult who keeps themself safe and makes wise choices.

For instance, you may have had an ATM card and used it when you were in high school, but your usage is likely to increase now because there are things you're paying for that you perhaps never had to pay for before, such as off-campus meals, clothing, and food and beverages to have at home in your dorm, apartment, or off-campus house. I hope you will take my advice to avoid using an ATM at night. If you have to get cash, use one inside a supermarket or go to a drive-through at your bank.

You need to go through your daily life knowing that there could be some potential danger out there today, every day, and plan things out so you can stay in the 90 percent of your personal safety zone. You need to prepare yourself, learn to predict risks, and do whatever you can to avoid becoming a victim of a crime, especially when you know you're about to leave the safety zone of your dorm room.

RISKS IN CARS AND BARS

One simple thing you can do to enhance your safety is to lock your car doors both when you leave it parked and when you return. Make sure that your key fob only unlocks your driver's side door and not the other doors. Once inside, lock your doors. If the automatic door lock feature stops working, please take it to the shop and get it fixed. Invest in your safety. That's planning and prevention. When you are home, manually lock your dorm room, apartment, or house doors from the inside to prevent break-ins or any unwanted visitors.

Try to avoid rough neighborhoods in the city. Anything could happen to your car, and you could get stranded and have to figure out how to get help. If you do get stranded, call for roadside service and stay in your car until help arrives. Don't interact with anyone outside your car unless it's the tow truck driver or roadside serviceperson.

Even when you are walking to your classes, stay aware of your surroundings. Remember to stay away from isolated, remote areas around the campus, and don't walk around alone at night. Believe it or not, even the library can be risky. Thieves will steal laptops and other valuables, and perverts will indecently expose themselves in the partially hidden areas of the bookshelves.

If you're going out to a bar, don't leave your drink uncovered. Some states now have laws that require bars to provide drink covers for patrons' drinks. If you are out somewhere that has drink covers, great, use them. But not all bars have them, so in most cases, you'll have to find another way to keep your drink safe. Using a paper napkin from the bar to put over your drink and holding the drink from the top will suffice to prevent anyone from spiking it. Ask a friend or a trustworthy person nearby to watch it for you, or better yet, just don't walk away from your drink.

RISKS ON PLANES AND TRAINS

Trains and buses have their own unique set of dangers. Don't let yourself fall asleep on a train or a bus, because who knows where you might end up. It might be a rough part of town or a very remote area. It's similar to when you get on a flight. When you arrive at the gate, make sure the gate is the right one, as sometimes gate changes happen from time to time.

One time, I was at the Boston Logan International Airport getting on an evening flight. I had glanced at my gate number on my phone a few hours before and remembered it. As I got to my gate, I found a good spot against the wall so I could see the gate and everyone around me. I had time to get on my laptop with my headset until I was ready to board. When it was time to board, I got in line, and when I approached the gate attendant, he told me I was at the wrong gate. I immediately looked at my phone and saw that they had changed my gate and it was on the other side of the terminal. When I got to my gate, the door was closed, and I missed my flight. Luckily, there happened to be another flight two hours later, but if there hadn't been, then I would have spent the night at the airport. The point of my story is to always check that you are at the right gate when you arrive for a flight. Also note that sometimes they can change your gate within forty-five minutes of boarding, so pay attention. You should do the same when you get on a bus or a train—make sure they will be stopping at your stop. Buses and trains sometimes have local routes and express routes. If the bus or train you're getting on is an express, it might not stop at your destination.

PERSONAL SAFETY ONLINE

It's not just when you're out and about that you need to think about these things. There are a lot of dangers involved in simply looking at your phone. There are scammers everywhere trying to steal your identity or your money or both. Online dating is a completely wild world these days. If you're meeting people online and then meeting up with them in person, you need to think about your safety from the very start. Make sure a friend knows where you're going and what time you'll be back. Don't give the person you're meeting too much personal information—like where you live or what your schedule is.

Catfishing is another problem. This is when someone pretends to be someone they're not, usually through an online connection. They can then lure you into a relationship with them and try to gain your trust to get you to give them money or share your identity or your secrets or to somehow steal from you. This has become extremely common these days. The good news is that there are strategies to help you avoid getting catfished. First, know the warning signs. Do they "love-bomb" you online but resist meeting you for an in-person date? Does their story not match what you can find online? Do they have a low amount of activity or followers on social media? These are all signs that they may not be who they say they are.

Recently, the dating app industry has been trying to make it as safe as possible to date online. For one thing, they've started providing opportunities for group meetups that allow you to pick and choose who you want to go out with in person rather than through pictures on your phone. Also, many of the apps now have verification strategies—such as face recognition and phone number or email confirmations. On Bumble, the women choose the men first, which can lead to more control of the process for women who are dating online.

I have a friend who spent six months only talking on the phone with the guy she matched with on the Bumble dating app. They did not meet for six months. They just talked. That is patience, right? She shared that she had a son with special needs, and he shared he had been married once and had five children from four different baby mamas. When she found that out, she asked if they could just talk on the phone for a while before meeting, and he respected her wishes. This woman was protecting her privacy and her life.

Social media has its own safety pitfalls. Most people know by now that you shouldn't post online that you're out of town, in case burglars somehow see that information and find out where you live. But other, more insidious things can happen. People can put up fake profiles and then try to connect with you or ask to be your friend, only to use the information in your profile to commit fraud or invade your privacy in some other way.

One time, someone had put a large cinder block inside a paper bag and placed it in the middle of the street. One of my husband's coworkers was driving through a neighborhood to get to a work-related site, and he saw the bag and thought it was just a paper bag in the street. He figured he could just run over it, and in doing so, the front right tire of his car was blown out by the cinder block. He stopped his car and noticed people from the neighborhood running over to try to rob him. Even though his car wasn't really too drivable, he managed to drive it out of the neighborhood and get help. The police mentioned to him that there had been a few incidents of this happening in that neighborhood and the people were robbed. We all want to be helpers out in the world, but you have to be cautious. If you are driving and pull into a parking lot and see someone lying on the ground, looking like they need help, don't jump out and help them. Be cautious—they could be tricking you and have accomplices in the bushes waiting to come out and gang up on you to steal your car—or you! You can just tell them, "I have the police on the phone, and help is on the way," and then drive away to a safe location. You never know; they could really be hurt, or they could be faking it, but either way, you're staying safe and helping them by calling for help from the authorities.

When I taught kids in r.a.d.KIDS classes, I would always tell them, "If someone you don't know asks you for help, don't go help them. Tell them you'll have your mom or dad or a trusted adult come help them. If someone is hurt, let the police or fire department help them because that's what they are trained to do. You did your part by calling for help."

DO YOUR RESEARCH

Different schools will have different levels of security. You can research how many campus police there are on the campus you're interested in or already attending. Larger schools are going to have a larger police force. Some schools might offer R.A.D. classes like the ones I used to teach at, while other schools may not offer them at all. Some schools will offer services for security guards or volunteers to escort students from class to your car if you have a night class, but not all schools do this. Check with the school of your choice. Do a deep dive into their safety protocols. These are things you should always consider when you are choosing a school and become knowledgeable about once you're there. Whatever security services your chosen school has, just be sure to take advantage of all the protection you can, and keep their number in your speed dial to call for help.

It may seem like a lot to think about in terms of personal safety, and I am giving you a laundry list here of all the most obvious ways you can avoid becoming a victim. Don't leave your backpack or your laptop lying around. Lock your dorm room, and if you don't have a lock for it, go get one and install it.

Here are the top four tips for success I give all students in my presentations:

1. Be alert to unusual or suspicious behavior.
2. Tell a trusted roommate/friend where you are going to be.
3. Call your campus security department if you need assistance or to report criminal activity.
4. Write down descriptions of the person(s) and license plate number(s) of any vehicles involved.

There's a saying that "things are not always as they seem." This is a great mindset to have when you're just out of the nest and into the wild. Just because a school looks quiet, peaceful, and safe doesn't mean there isn't any crime there. Just because a person looks honest doesn't mean they are. Just because the plans for an outdoor adventure in a remote area sound fun doesn't mean it will necessarily be safe. Do your homework—and not just for your classes. Find out as much as you can about the people you're interacting with and the places you're going. Just interact and be friendly, and ask questions without sounding nosy and getting into their business. Be proactive when making sure the plans you're participating in will be both enjoyable and safe.

In the late 1980s, an important law was passed to address the problem of transparency around college crime. The law has been amended with improvements and additions over the years, but the essence remains the same.

Unfortunately, the law was born from a tragic crime. Years ago, in 1986, a nineteen-year-old student at Lehigh University in Pennsylvania was raped and killed by another student. The victim's name was Jeanne Clery, and as a result of these events, the Jeanne Clery Campus Safety Act was established to mandate that all universities that offer financial aid must extensively report and make public the crime statistics on and around their campuses. These crimes include rape, assault, and theft, but also more campus-specific activities such as hazing. For you, this means that you can access the crime statistics of almost any school in the US and you can compare crime statistics between one school and another when making decisions about where to attend college.

If it is discovered that the full extent of all crime statistics has not been reported by one of these universities, the school will receive heavy penalties, with fines in the hundreds of thousands of dollars. This accountability is an important positive step in our higher education system and goes a long way toward keeping kids safe on campus. Colleges and universities now have to file daily crime reports on all campuses as well as send out emergency notifications to all students and staff if a crime has occurred. They have to publish an annual security report that includes all reports of dating violence, domestic violence, sexual assault, stalking, and hazing.

It's wild out there. A lot of violence, destruction, and aggressive behavior can happen, and there have been some tragic outcomes on campuses over the years. I don't want to scare you and turn you into an agoraphobic who stays in their dorm room 24/7. I just want to educate you, inform you, and prepare you for reality. Be aware of how to protect your personal safety so that you can make your transition out of the nest a smooth and pain-free experience. You're on the brink of all the magic that awaits you in your life. Why not protect that future and make sure it's not tainted by bad experiences?

Lili was book smart, but she wasn't street smart. She was in her White Color Code, oblivious to any risks that may have lain ahead. If you don't stay A.W.A.R.E. and in your alert yet relaxed Yellow Color Code, especially when you are out and about, on and off campus, you can still become a victim of a crime no matter how advanced you are in your knowledge of self-defense and crime prevention.

College campuses are known to hold new dangers for the college-aged young adult, and one of the common dangers is the situation Lili found herself in as a rape victim. Cases of "date rape" are all too common on campuses and among young adults in any circumstances. That's why it's so crucial for young adults to fully understand what constitutes consent and to be aware of the laws around sexual assault. In the next chapter, we will face the unshakable truth that no means no and discuss some of the ways this truth is tested among young adults.

CHAPTER 9: STAY A.W.A.R.E. TAKEAWAYS

- Think about your safety no matter where you are, even online.
- Keep your car locked even when you're inside, and cover your drink when you're in a bar.
- Make good choices!

NO MEANS NO

Several years ago, a video went viral, and in it, a stick figure asks another stick figure if they want a cup of hot tea. The video shows all the different scenarios for several different answers the other stick figure might give. If the guest stick figure says "Yes, please" enthusiastically, then the narrator tells us that the host should make them the tea and give them the tea, but they should not pour it down their throat. If the guest says, "I don't know if I want tea or not," then the host can make them the tea if they want but should not be surprised or upset if they don't drink it. And they definitely should not pour the tea down their throat. If the guest says, "No, I don't want tea," then the host stick figure should not make them tea, not give them tea, and not pour it down their throat. If the guest initially wants tea but then changes their mind and doesn't want tea, the host should not make them drink the tea and definitely not pour it down their throat. If the guest is unconscious at any point in the visit, the host should not pour the tea down their throat.

Unconscious people don't like tea, the narrator explains.

You can watch the "Tea Consent" video, youtube.com/watch?v=fGoWLWS4-kU, right now if you like, but you get the idea.

It doesn't matter if you change your mind. That's your choice and your right. In the video, the guest says, "Sure, I'd like some tea," and then the host goes through all of the steps to make the tea. He boils the water, brews the tea, and takes it over to the guest. But then the guest says, "Hang on, no, I'm not ready for tea." The host is frustrated because he spent all this time making the tea only for them to change their mind and say they don't want it anymore. Well, as we see in the video, that's too bad. You can't shove tea down someone's throat.

You can learn a lot about the concept of consent from this video. If you think about it, Lili was forced to "drink tea" while she was unconscious and never had the chance to give consent.

The moral of this story is that you should never force anything on anyone, and you should know that if someone forces anything on you, you have rights. This chapter is about the complex topic of rape, which is nonconsensual sexual intercourse. It's also about sexual assault, which is nonconsensual sexual interactions of any kind, not including intercourse. It would take volumes to explore the whole topic because, even though it may seem simple, it's often difficult for people to understand that no really means no, no matter what. If someone says yes and then changes their mind to no, no means no. If someone said yes to that for the last twelve days but then says no on the thirteenth day, no means no. If someone says yes and then, even in the middle of intercourse, says no, no still means no. It could be your spouse, your boyfriend, or just someone you're dating. If you say no, it means no. It is illegal and punishable in a court of law for anyone to have sex with you without your permission.

Before we go on, I want to say that this is the most difficult and emotionally charged chapter of the book. But I saved it for last because it is the most important, and everything that has come before in the previous chapters was laying the groundwork for this topic. It is the most serious chapter, and that is simply because there are incredibly serious consequences for crossing the line between consensual and nonconsensual sexual activity.

A "DATE" RAPE STORY

I remember, one time, there was a man who wanted to do a ride-along with our police department because he thought he might be interested in working in law enforcement. At the time, it was my role at the police department to run background checks on people wanting to do a ride-along. I ran this man's background, and he was good to go. When I called to schedule his ride-along, he had just started a new job and wanted to wait a bit until he could get his schedule together, and he would get back to me. He called me back a few months later and told me he was ready, and instead of running another background check on him, I scheduled him, with the assumption that nothing had changed in his background. Well, I was wrong. I assumed he was still fine and scheduled him for his ride-along. The day after his ride-along, one of the officers sent me an email telling me that this man had been arrested and asked why I scheduled him. Rut-roh! Apparently, between the time that I had run his background check and the day he was scheduled for his ride-along, he had gone out on a date with a coworker, they were sitting in his car, and she tried to get out, but he wouldn't let her. He kept her in there and was forcing her to let him kiss her and fondle her. He didn't hurt her, but he trapped her in the car, and she couldn't get out.

Finally, she got out of the car, went to her house, called her ex-boyfriend, and told him what had happened. He told her to go to the police and file a kidnapping case, which she did, and soon police officers picked him up while at his job and put him in jail. Had I run his background check the second time, I would have seen this arrest and not let him go on a ride-along.

Later, I learned that the ride-along kept harassing the officer to check his record, and the officer was getting a little suspicious, so they drove back to the station, and the officer had the ride-along sit and wait in the lobby. When the officer returned, he told the ride-along, "Son, your ride-along is over. You can go home now." The ride-along asked why, and the officer said, "You know why." The officer had seen that the ride-along was arrested for false imprisonment.

Oddly, the man went out of his way to ask whether there was anything on his record. He must not have realized that if you go to jail, it always goes on your record. When you are arrested for anything, it goes on your record. You are issued a personal file number (PFN), which is an identifying number for all arrested suspects. This man "only" made out with this woman, but something as simple as not letting her go got him arrested, as it would anyone who holds someone against their will. She was not giving consent; it was as simple as that. That is one end of the spectrum, but on the other end, you have something as tragic, traumatic, and life-altering as what happened to Lili, who was raped while she was unconscious and never even had a chance to say yes or no.

There's a sad misconception in the world today about something called "date" rape. What is date rape? Is it rape?

Yes, it is rape. So why do we try to soften it by calling it "date" rape? How does the fact that you know someone make it any less serious or harmful? It's certainly against the law just as much as rape that isn't between two people who are dating. If someone was going out with you and they murdered you, would you want that to be called "date" murder? No. Murder is murder, rape is rape, and no—you guessed it—is no.

In the R.A.D. manual I use in my trainings, the writers state, "All rape is equally criminal and equally important to defend against."

You're new to college, and there's so much to learn at once. I get it, but if you can just take one thing away from reading this book, it's this: don't force anyone to do something they don't want to do. This applies to getting people to drink or go somewhere they're not interested in, and it definitely applies to sexual activity.

Sadly, many families are still raising their sons to think of having sex with a woman as something they are entitled to and something a woman is obligated to give them (if she's beautiful, or if she's flirty, or if she has a crush on you, or if any other false reason comes into play), but that is simply not true. Everyone has the right to say no to sex, and trying to have sex with someone who doesn't want to is a felony in a court of law and will land you in prison. You have to know how to draw the line at forcing yourself on someone else. And of course, while most rapes consist of a man forcing himself on a woman, sometimes it's the other way.

I read a story several years ago about a boy who was raised by his mother, and he raped a girl, not knowing that he was raping her or that it was wrong, because he had never been taught this truth. Whether he was informed and educated about this did not matter one bit because he still went to trial, and he still went to jail. For ten years. This young man was angry at the system because no one had taught him that no means no.

Another boy who was an only child raised by his single mother in New York was accused of not only rape but also killing someone in Central Park. He brought a girl out into the park, and she assumed they were just going to hang out. He ended up raping her and choking her to death. He apparently thought his mother could get him out of it. In court, he claimed he had no idea that it was a crime. "Nobody told me that 'no' means 'no,'" he said.

Moms, if you're reading this, ask yourself whether you want your son to serve time in jail for rape. If not, then make sure they are fully aware that forcing themselves on a woman is against the law and comes with a prison sentence. And everyone also needs to understand what is defined as rape, and what is not, and that there are serious ramifications for the crime.

You may think rape is only when a stranger violently assaults a woman and has intercourse with her. That certainly is one definition of rape, and of course, it is punishable by law. But rape is *any* instance of nonconsensual sexual intercourse between two people. It can be a man and a woman, two women, or two men. While this is rare, rape can be between a woman and a man when it's the woman who forces the man to have sex.

Rape can be between a woman and her spouse or boyfriend. As we saw in the "Tea Consent" video, just because someone has said yes for years, it doesn't mean that if they say no today, you can force them to have sex with you. Just because you've been on a date with someone all night and it's your sixth date doesn't mean you can force them to have sex with you.

There is absolutely no circumstance in which it is acceptable or legal to force someone to have sex with you.

STALKERS

No also means no when it comes to stalking, which is punishable by law as well. Stalkers can be quietly watching you and doing no harm, or they can get aggressive and try to destroy your life. Some even end up murdering their victims. In 2011, Michelle Le, a nursing student at Hayward Kaiser, was stalked and murdered by her friend who was jealous that Michelle had allegedly dated her ex-boyfriend.

The lesson is to be aware of the signs of stalking and know how to recognize when someone is stalking you.

What are the signs? If someone shows up somewhere where you are, and you haven't directly told them you're going to be there, they might be stalking you. If they are sending unwanted communication through the phone, email, text, or snail mail, they are stalking you. If someone is constantly showing up in places in a way that feels like they're following you, they might be stalking you. Any kind of threats, spreading of rumors, or surveillance and anything that feels obsessive can be stalking.

WHAT EXACTLY IS CONSENT?

When it comes to sexual acts, consent is basically just an understanding between two people that it's okay to engage in a sexual activity. If someone is impaired in any way, shape, or form, no matter what they say, then there is no consent. Of course, if they simply say "No, I'm not ready" or just plain "No," then of course there is no consent there either.

Consent means both people openly agree to have sexual relations. If one of them changes their mind and asserts that no, they don't want to, then the other person just has to live with it. They will have to deal with their desires in another way.

What if a woman is afraid to say no? What happens then? For instance, if two people are engaging in foreplay, and the girl reaches a point where she doesn't want to go any further, she might be afraid to say no. She goes ahead and gives consent, but afterward, she might claim that she was raped that night. At this point, it becomes her word against his.

Whole lives are at stake on this issue of rape, so if you are accusing someone of it, you had better be sure that it actually happened the way you say it did. Kids in high school can get expelled, kicked off their sports team, and have a dark spot on their record for life if they are arrested for a sex offense. Young college-aged men will have the same consequences. Once you're out in the workforce, being labeled as a sex offender is a serious black mark on your record. You will lose out on a lot of jobs and opportunities.

The best piece of advice I can give you is for both the males and the females reading this book: if you're not sure, then don't do it. Guys, if you're not sure she's ready and willing, then don't do it, and especially if she says no, do not proceed. Gals, if you're not sure you're ready and willing, then don't do it, and make your "no" as loud and clear as you can. Yes, the burden of that part is on you, but guys have an equal burden, and that's to be aware of the signals a woman is sending and to respect those signals, whether they are verbal or not.

Let's say our friend Bri was flirting at a party and gave the guy she was flirting with a lot of signals that she wanted to sleep with him. He asked if she wanted to go back to his room with him, and she said yes. He asked her to take off some of her clothes in his room, and she went ahead and did it without a word. Then he starts making the moves to have intercourse with her. Is she obligated to go ahead with it just because she sent those signals? Of course not.

The difference in penalties for sexual assault as opposed to rape is proof of this. In most states, regardless of whether there needs to be consent or not, rape is a felony, while sexual assault is often a Class A misdemeanor, but it still can carry up to nine months in jail and up to a $10,000 fine.

Anyone with common sense knows that intercourse is far more serious than just fooling around. For young people, it can have serious life-changing complications, such as pregnancy. It can also easily give someone a sexually transmitted disease. The laws on rape vary widely from state to state. Some states only perceive coercive penetration as rape. This means that consent isn't the issue; coercion is.

If you are unsure whether you want to have sex with someone, it is a sign that you're not ready. If you are listening to your intuition, you're going to know "deep down" whether you're ready, and sometimes you'll be able to sense whether the other person is ready too.

If you want something real, it's worth the wait. This is a complicated topic, and it's made even more complex by gender differences in the way sex is perceived. Women and men view sex differently, and they feel differently about the act. This has to be acknowledged by both sides. And if men can understand that for women, sex can be more of an emotional act, requiring an emotional commitment, then men can be more attuned to that and act accordingly.

THE CHIP CHALLENGE

Do not force anything on anyone, ever. The consequences of sexually transmitted diseases and/or pregnancy from sexual intercourse can be devastating.

Every fall, from 2016 to 2023, the One-Chip Challenge would appear on social media, encouraging viewers to eat chips seasoned with Carolina Reaper chiles, manufactured by Paqui. These chips were extremely hot, especially if you were not accustomed to heat in your food—but even if you were, your mouth would burn painfully for hours after eating just a few bites of one of these chips. Later, it was discovered that the spice inside could have health consequences because it was so potent. People could get organ damage or have a heart attack from eating one of the chips. Many people were eating them out of peer pressure, and after one teenager died from eating one, partially because he had existing heart problems that were greatly exacerbated by the heat of the chip, the manufacturer eventually removed them from the shelves. Can you imagine if someone had forced one of those on you, and suddenly you were in burning pain and possibly injured for life? Or dead?

Pouring hot tea down someone's throat, daring them to eat a Reaper chip, or forcing unwanted sex are just different versions of the same thing: violating, aggressive acts that will hurt another person.

We've come to the end of this personal safety guide. But this is just the beginning of a bright future for you and your loved ones! May your young adult years be filled with learning, growth, fun, friendship, love, and laughter. Armed with the tools in this book to do everything in your power to stay safe and support the safety of others, you are ready for your college years, your journey into the workplace, and the rest of your life.

CHAPTER 10: STAY A.W.A.R.E. TAKEAWAYS

- No means no. It's against the law to force anyone to have sex against their will. It's a serious offence and comes with serious consequences.
- Consent is key; without it, you are breaking the law.
- Don't ever force someone to do something they don't want to do.

CONCLUSION

Personal safety may not be the most fun-filled subject, and it's not meant to be. It is a serious subject, and I want you to take it seriously. I wrote this book to help young people like you become fluent in the language of self-defense and to encourage you to stay A.W.A.R.E. I hope you will carry the knowledge in these pages with you as you navigate the wild of young adulthood during your college-age years. The more you can avoid becoming a victim, the more fun you can have out there.

Your goals during this time of your life are becoming clearer as you learn more and more about the world. This is a time for growth, and it's also meant to be filled with good times. I believe the best way to have those outcomes is to take your personal safety very seriously so you're free to enjoy all that life has to offer.

To ensure that the risks and dangers of life outside the nest don't get in the way of your learning and enjoying life to the fullest, you now realize the vast majority of your safety lies in your ability to stay A.W.A.R.E.

This means knowing what color code you're in and taking all of the precautions needed as you navigate your new environment and your newfound freedom. This way, you will stay in your Yellow Color Code.

Know the A.W.A.R.E. mindset:

- Stay **Alert** at all times.
- **Watch** what's going on around you.
- **Assess** the situation.
- **Respond** to potential danger.
- **Escape** if necessary.

Not only that, but you're also going to stay mindful of when you might be allowing a perpetrator of a crime to turn you into a victim of a crime. You're going to remove any opportunities you can to keep that from happening.

If you get into trouble and, for some reason, can't escape, you'll know how to use your personal weapons to disarm and disable an assailant quickly and safely so that you can make your escape.

Either way, you'll also be a good witness, taking note of as many details as possible and not trying to be a hero, so that law enforcement can do what it's meant to: find and apprehend the suspect.

One of the most important concepts I hope you'll keep with you forever is the value of your intuition. Your instinctual feelings of fear or apprehension are sending you a clear message that something is not quite right. In those times, you're also going to think like a LEO, using strategies and tactics of law enforcement, like placing yourself in the safest position, calling for help rather than going in alone, and staying on top of threats by keeping an eye out for any suspicious behavior in your surroundings.

After reading this book, but also out in the wild world, enjoy all life has to offer and avoid danger like a pro. When it comes to rape and sexual assault, you're now armed with knowledge about the laws and clarity on how to avoid ever becoming a victim of a sex offense. You understand that no means no and that forceful, nonconsensual sexual aggression is a very serious crime.

Your next steps now are to put the numbers of your local law enforcement agencies in your phone and to research the crime statistics of the town you're in and the campus you're on, if applicable. You're also going to buy a couple of pepper sprays or similar legal self-defense sprays and use one to learn how to operate and save the other for any emergencies. You're going to check your college campus or local area for any R.A.D. classes or self-defense classes if you want to enhance your self-defense knowledge. You're never going to leave your valuables in your car, walk into a dark parking structure late at night, ignore your gut feelings of fear, or let yourself go into the White Color Code of oblivion to risks or the Black of overwhelming, paralyzing fright.

These and other simple yet powerful strategies to avoid becoming a victim can truly change your life. If you embrace the reality that the wild world can be unpredictable, stay cautious, and make smart choices, you'll steer clear of dangerous situations.

Finally, this book is meant to be shared. I encourage you to pass it along to your friends and family. Hopefully, they will be better listeners and learners about personal safety than some of my relatives! Kidding, not kidding. The more people who understand these fundamental but essential principles, the safer our world can become.

At the back of this book, you will find a list of resources

dedicated to crime prevention, reporting, and opportunities for further self-defense training.

Remember, you are ultimately in charge of your own safety. Stay A.W.A.R.E., stay safe, and stay empowered. I wish you success on your life journey to staying safe!

ACKNOWLEDGMENTS

A special thank-you to my publishing and graphic team, Candace Read, Anna Dorfman, and Katie Lathrop, for supporting my vision and helping me transform it into a "must-read" playbook for young adults who are leaving the nest and going into the wild. Your expertise elevated this project far beyond what I imagined.

To my illustration and photography team—my sister Desiree Bustamante—who has the talent to bring any illustration to life! To Dave Cruz, professional photographer, www.davecruz.com.

To my film crew—Marissa Bustamante, Kelsey Marasigan, and Brandon Shores—whose shoulders I tapped to help me with this project and who helped create a live version of being a good witness.

I could not have written and published this book if it weren't for the full support and permission from founder and CEO of R.A.D. Systems, Larry Nadeau. And to all the others who have helped me get here, including Emelyn dela Peña and all the R.A.D. instructors that I have met and taught with since 2000. Your dedication to personal safety and commitment to educating students on college campuses and in communities across the country continue to inspire me. You rock!

To my LECT (law enforcement consultant team), as I proudly call them—Michael DeOrian of the Hayward Police Department; Mike Elder of the Cal State University, East Bay Police Department; Kevin Gonzales (Ret.) of the Cal State University, East Bay Police Department; Jason Martinez (Ret.) of the Hayward Police Department; Bryan Matthews of the Hayward Police Department; Thomas Trester (Ret.) of the Fresno County Sheriff's Office; Joe Whitson (Ret.) of the Osceola County Sheriff's Office; and Dan Willis (Ret.) of the La Mesa Police Department—thank you for all your time in helping me with information gathering, fact-checking, and ensuring that the terminology, events, and details in this book were represented as accurately as possible.

A big shout-out to the Chandler Police Department's R.A.D. program, where I was able to continue teaching self-defense when I retired and moved to Arizona.

Last but not least, to my husband, for allowing me to take a leap of faith and supporting me in my true calling to write this book.

ABOUT THE AUTHOR

S. GALE BLETH was born in Oakland, California, and grew up a military brat, moving from coast to coast across the country throughout her childhood. She spent parts of her early life in Connecticut, Alaska, and Puerto Rico, and eventually her family moved back to California, where she graduated high school. Gale went on to earn her bachelor's degree in speech communication from California State University, East Bay (formerly Hayward) and later received her master's degree in leadership from Saint Mary's College in Moraga, California.

Gale's professional career includes sixteen years at California State University, East Bay, where she worked closely with student organizations and partnered with the university police department. She has been a certified R.A.D. Systems self-defense instructor since 2000 and served for sixteen years as a crime prevention specialist for the Hayward Police Department, teaching personal safety to the Hayward community. She is a retired state board president of the California Crime Prevention Officers' Association (CCPOA) from 2018 to 2025. Gale's passion has always been to empower people and help them change their mindset about their own personal safety. Early in her self-defense teachings, her participants shared how their awareness and confidence had grown under her guidance and enabled them to always be aware of their surroundings. After many years of teaching people of all age groups to take their personal safety to another level, Gale felt the calling to expand the A.W.A.R.E. mindset and share her experience and knowledge with the world.

She would love to hear from you! You can email her at info@stay-aware.com or visit her website at Stay-Aware.com.